Magic of the Nc

Dedicated
To my partner Stuart Littlejohn

And
To Robert Henry
*A magical brother who walked into the West on Dec 25th
2012*

Josephine McCarthy

Magic of the North Gate

By same author

Magical Knowledge Book I - Foundations/The Lone Practitioner
Magical Knowledge Book II - The Initiate
Magical Knowledge Book III - Contact of the Adepts

Contents

Acknowledgements

Thanks to the following people who all inspire me, bully me and keep an eye on me: Cecilia Lindley, Toni Paris, Anthony Thompson, John Plummer, Christin Cleaver, Frater Acher, Karen McKeown. A special thankyou to Paolo Sammut, a magical co worker who was kind enough to look over the mss for me, and to Mogg Morgan for being a wonderful publisher and all round great guy. I also want to give a special thanks to my partner Stuart Littlejohn, a vastly talented man who has endless patience and a wicked sense of humour.

Foreword

By Frater Acher

Before you dive into the depths of the magical teaching, techniques and wisdom this book offers, I recommend that you ask yourself a very simple question. It is so simple that it might be considered the most essential question of magical practice at all: 'Why use Magic?' Being truthful and honest with yourself why you are using magic is not only important for defining your own magical path; it is maybe even more important because the first thing that any spiritual being will look at is your magical intent.

Ten years ago if someone had asked me why I walk the path of magic I would have answered 'to gain conscious knowledge and conversation with my Holy Guardian Angel'. Maybe I would have hesitated and then added: 'Oh, and of course to discover my True Will!' Today, I don't think either of the two are relevant answers.

Today I think of this essential question as a Zen koan. It looks deceitfully simple at first glance. Yet, if you were to approach your Zen teacher with your intuitive answer, there is a high chance he would smile and turn you away. So you would return to your meditation place and meditate over this most simple question again. 'What possibly could have been wrong with my answer? Isn't contact with my Holy Guardian Angel a most worthy goal in life? Isn't peeling away layer after layer of ego-driven wishes and desires to finally find and fulfil my True Will what drove mages for at least... well, at least since Crowley succeeded to establish the highly ambiguous term 'True Will' as the most successful fig leaf since the philosophy of hedonism to turn your life into a self-centred journey of narcissism...? So what is wrong with my answer?'

Well, that is exactly the question we need to ask ourselves: what can possibly be wrong with such a simple answer to such a simple question? To be honest, I spent most of the last two years searching for a better one, an answer that passes with approval by the Zen teacher we call Life.

I guess Life doesn't like this answer, because it works against a much broader horizon than I or most other humans normally do. Life simply isn't confined by the limits we often take for granted and it doesn't need to break down its lessons into chapters by years or decades like we do. It is free to perceive obvious and painful challenges we encounter as essentially positive and deeply enriching, and it is never driven by angst or fear like we as humans will always be to a certain extent.

Life, being what it is, doesn't even bother too much about my personal conditions or reasons for giving this answer? In fact, Life again might have a much broader frame of reference when asking the question 'Why use Magic?'... Let's use a little role play to illustrate how Life might look at this question.

For a moment let's swap roles between the spirits we tend to work with in magic, and us as humans. Let's listen to Life as it poses a very similar question to these spirits or even to our very own HGA: 'Why use Humans?' And as our HGA looks completely gob smacked, Life goes on to say: 'Look, it takes years of dedicated hard work with a single human being to train them on the most basic steps like how to deal with large amounts of energy, how to talk to us, how to be okay with not seeing us on the physical plane, etc. It takes all this effort to raise humans to the essential level where they can actually be of help. And then what? How many humans have you seen who - once they reach this threshold of understanding and power - actually offer themselves up in service, who let go of their personal agenda, of their human wishes and desires, of their dreams of individual eternity, of personal remembrance by their offspring, and - worst of all - of their deeply engrained craving to experience god-like significance?' 'Well', the spirit would turn away from its Zen teacher and ponder, 'truth be told, I haven't exactly seen a lot of humans like this...' So why use humans?

My point, I guess, is quite straight forward. As long as our answer to 'Why use Magic?' revolves around ourselves as the central pillar of our universe, we can't expect Life to have any specific interest in it. Because whether we fail or succeed doesn't matter to anybody but ourselves. If this is good enough for you - go right ahead. Many generations of magicians went ahead before and I fear many more will follow.

When I draw a line under the dozens and dozens of magical training manuals I have read and practiced on in my life, what remains is some highly powerful, many average and a lot of feeble techniques to optimize yourself and the narrow world you call your life. Most of these books give you techniques to engineer yourself into a better version of yourself: to grow from Neophyte to Zelator to Adept to Magister; to continuously over your life-time climb a rung of the eternal Hermetic Ladder of self-improvement, one step at a time. The aim is to one day finally emerge as the master of all arcane disciplines, the stone of the wise, impersonated in a suit of flesh and bones that you can be proud to call yourself.

Don't get me wrong. I followed this path for more than a decade intensely, practicing everyday for hours like many of us did or still do.

And I still believe the motivation to climb this ladder is a wonderful motive to set out on the magical path when we are young or start out completely fresh. But... there comes a time, there comes a point in our lives as magicians when we have climbed this ladder high enough, when we need to ask ourselves if this original motive still holds true? Is it still good enough, to simply focus on ourselves, given all the things we have gained through the support of spirits and divine beings way beyond our capacities? In other words: at which point do we owe back to life and all its forces that helped us become who we are?

If every spirit you have ever worked with was allowed to direct one wish at you - what would they ask for? How would this long list read? And how many of these wishes have you fulfilled so far? The most essential question I can think of for us as magicians to answer is 'Why use Magic?' Whatever answer we come up with, it should also answer the question Life might pose to the spirits: 'Why use Humans?'

How long do we give ourselves to realize that the ladder we were feverishly climbing in reality is not only a ladder, but is also a chain: it is the Hermetic or Golden Chain, the one that connects all beings, small and large, weak and powerful, through threads of life and power. The question I needed to ask myself was: How long do I give myself to find my place in this chain - and when should I start working not my own agenda, but on the ones that matter beyond me?

I don't know where you are on your magical path. But before you set out to read this book you may want to take a moment to pause and reflect. To ask yourself: 'Am I still a seedling or am I a tree?' 'And if it is the latter, who has come to shelter in my shadow? Who eats from my fruits? Which nests am I ready to host in my crown?'

It doesn't mean I'll stop growing, stop following the cycles of the year and refresh myself with water and air and light everyday. It simply means that even after all these intense years of work on myself, this work will continue; yet it will change from a mean to its own end into a basis from which I can begin to give back.

A couple of essential questions you might want to consider as you are approaching the teachings and techniques of this wonderful book could be the following:

'Do I know what the stones, plants and earth in my garden desire?

Am I aware of the needs of the fairy beings and spirits who live with me in this house?'

'Do I have favours to return to spirits who have helped me in the past?'

'Are there spirits unacknowledged in my personal realm (body, house, community) who are asking for service?'

'Which physical world events might have impacted spirits living in this land with me negatively? Are there ways I can help or support?'

'What do my dreams teach me about jobs I can be useful in - through the tool I have turned myself into?'

If everything goes right to plan we not necessarily move from student to teacher, but often from student to servant.

Frater Acher
Munich 2013

Introduction

Many years ago as a young budding magician, I scoffed at a piece of wisdom that was offered to me, a true wisdom that I was too young to grasp. The woman who was my mentor at that time was talking to me about the directions and the powers that flow from the directions. She said, "You can only really master the skills of one direction in a lifetime". Hmph. I had been working with the directions and had strong contacts in all four of them. I had passed over the threshold of all four directions and explored the inner realms that were filtered by those directions. She was wrong, I thought. And I was arrogant as well as ignorant.

Many things she dropped in my lap in my twenties only began to dawn upon me years later and many of her wisdoms that I swept to one side as 'quaint' or 'of their time' eventually revealed themselves to me over many years. The depth and knowledge of those insights astounds me and I truly wish with all my heart she was still alive so I could go back to sit in her front room which was heavily decorated with tons of Egyptian bling, and say, "I apologise for being a stupid arrogant young woman".

She was right. The levels of knowledge, contact and power that can be connected with in any one direction, plus the skills to learn how to wield that power take a lifetime to learn. When she talked about 'outer court' learning, I assumed she meant learning tarot, outer drama/ritual, setting up altars, astrology etc, and when she mentioned 'inner court' work, she meant astral work. And that would be the understanding of most magicians. It was certainly my understanding for many years.

But the dawn came slowly that the 'outer court' in my understanding, was not a court even... it was merely the path leading to the court. The inner visionary work in temples, Underworlds etc was the 'outer court' work (even though it is conducted in the inner worlds). The veil was slowly being pulled back to show me another layer, another 'court' of the Great Work (service to the land and Divinity) a completely other level of contact and power.

I began to work with this new layer I had been exposed to. I didn't fully understand it, I could not form it no matter how I tried and I found I could not express it; basically because I really did not understand it. The deeper I stepped into this newly found 'court', the less I understood and the more and more I came to realise that the work I had been doing for so long, which I considered to be 'deep', was not really even scratching the surface.

Inner Contacts tried various ways to show me how to work, how to form this power, how to connect with the levels of consciousness, but I really was not getting it. I was trying to fall back on old comforts, systems that I already knew and understood: I was being talked to in a new language and I was trying to translate rather than simply learn the new language.

Over a five year span my connection to and contact with this new layer drifted in and out. I did not know how to consciously apply this dynamic; I didn't even have a name for it. In the end I surrendered and just let it flow naturally. The power flowed through a specific filter: a direction. And by direction/element I don't mean that the power only came from place, rather it was filtered through a specific magical power filter: a magical elemental direction.

I had worked with this power filter for many years as part of a four direction pattern and all the while I thought I was learning about the powers in that direction when in fact I was only building the filter through which that power could pass.

The reason I am telling you all of this is to show you how magic reveals itself. When you first make contact with inner beings and power, and you have an 'experience', you think you are the 'bees knees' or some people go all 'messiah'. A decade or two down the road you get knocked around a lot and realise just how much there is to magic and how unwieldy it can be, but also how beautiful. You do rituals, visions, initiations and settle in to 'being a magician'.

And then one day, a decade or two further again, slowly, silently, another veil is drawn back: it is like looking out at the universe, at the endless flow of stars for the very first time. Its magnificence and vastness overwhelm you as you realise that you have only learned the first letter of the alphabet; you have a very long way to go before you can begin to write poetry.

This book is about that first and most powerful letter in the alphabet, the powers that flow from specific sources, powers that run through our world and trigger the formation of magical and religious structures. It is viewed in this book via our work on the land, our bodies, the elements and directions, and our own mortality.

This is not a beginner book, rather is it a book of techniques and methods for working magicians, priestesses and occultists, techniques that take us deeper into magic and therefore ourselves. This is about how that power flows, what it does, how it organises itself, what it can become for good or bad and how it can all go horribly wrong.

1

The Body and Magic

Keeping body and
soul together in the crucible of magic

The most important thing to remember before we delve into the depths of how magic affects the mind and body is the necessity to put this information in perspective. Yes magic does affect the mind and body once the magician starts to work in any depth, but knowing those affects, knowing the warning signs and acting accordingly ensures that the changes become a part of the path of the magician and not a passive consequence of action. There are many things that a magician can do to minimise the effects of magic upon their bodies and use the power flowing through them to bring about balance within themselves. Also, acting in full knowledge of the possible consequences of a magical action enables the magician to make better informed choices, and to recognise the various stages of development that they are going through.

When the magician/occultist/priestess reaches a certain level of skill and action, the power being moved around is often enough for it to start to have an effect upon the practitioner's body. Magic is about change and change often brings things with it that we find uncomfortable on many levels. As we delve into working with power, the areas within our bodies and minds that are weak, unbalanced or toxic begin to galvanise into action. Magic, among other things, is a catalyst for change and the change comes through us before it goes out into the world. Anything within us that is imbalanced reacts to the energy that is worked with in ritual and vision and a process of change occurs for good or bad depending upon what magical action is taken.

Whether that change will be productive or destructive is largely dependant upon what energy/power it is that you are working with and how you react to the impact of that work. If you recognise the imbalance and address it, then the interaction between the magical energy and your body is ultimately productive, however uncomfortable it may be as an initial process.

If you resist the change brought about by the catalyst action then it will ultimately become destructive. It is akin to ignoring rising flood waters behind a dam and not directing it down safe channels. Many very successful and powerful magicians/occultists I know have gone through massive change as a result of their magic. For example the change can manifest as the body not being able to tolerate poisons or toxins any longer: the magician finds they can no longer get away with heavy drinking, toxic eating etc. Their sleep changes, their dreams change, and their consciousness matures. The initial impact of this shift in how the body and mind operates can sometimes appear to be debilitating in the short term but the magician emerges out of that initial 'healing crisis' much stronger and better balanced.

As a former ballet dancer/coach, I observe it in magicians as a similar process to dancers when they shift from being amateur dancers to professionals for the first time. The huge increase in workload on the body and mind is a shock to most new professionals and it takes the body and mind a good six months to adjust to the new energetic, dietary, emotional and life changes that are demanded of a professional dancer. And so it is with magicians once they step onto the road of serious work.

Anything that we do to push our physical, intellectual or spiritual boundaries is going to have an impact for both good and bad upon our bodies. It is the reality of exploration and of working with power. The key is to work with the burdens to develop endurance properly, like an athlete.

Magic in its depth creates boundaries of energetic opposition and tension; it is part and parcel of how power works – it also protects the integrity of the inner worlds as well as beefing up the magician. If someone is a mindless idiot and is playing around with magic, when they hit an obstruction they usually quit and move on to something else that is easier.

Another type of idiot (I was once that idiot) would run at the obstruction with the intent to smash it down. It tends to hurt when you do that. A sensible magician would observe the boundary, figure out what it was doing, learn how it works, why it was there, what is beyond it, what beings operate with and around it etc. They would carefully work very close to the obstruction, and then build up a form of communication with it. Using that method, you learn a lot, you get stronger and finally, the obstruction slowly dismantles so that you can continue on your path of work.

As you work closely with a magical obstruction/block/locked door, not only does it give you time to learn about the obstruction, it gives your body time to adjust to the power around it. If your body is fit and healthy, it will quickly adjust to the different power, leaving no or little ill effect. If you blast through an obstruction, you will find yourself either very bruised and you will be booted out of the inner worlds, or you will expose yourself to an immense amount of power that your body is not prepared to handle.

These obstructions are part of magical learning and it is a phenomenon that occurs whether you work in ritual, vision or both. They can manifest as total blocks in the work, so a ritual pattern will suddenly not work and everything will shut down, or in vision it can appear as literally a block or a guardian that slings you out of wherever you were working. Either way, using either method or both combined, it does have an impact upon your body and mind when you hit these walls, and it is a signal that you are on a threshold of leaping forward in your work, but that you need to back up, slow down and learn something first. It can also act as an idiot filter: it discourages stupid people so that they will go back to playing with crystals and silly outfits.

This was understood in earlier times when magic was a major part of religion in the ancient world and fragments of that understanding can still be found today in some religions. Priests and priestesses of the mystery religions were trained not only in their magical and spiritual crafts, but also in the physical disciplines necessary to maintain strength and health while mediating and interacting with power. Often the physical training would be the first part of a young person's training to get the body in a state of peak strength and discipline.

Diet also played a major role in many mystery disciplines and fragments of those disciplines have stayed with us today in the form of religious dietary taboos. Because so much information was lost in the West when Christianity swept through Europe, we have to piece back together as much knowledge as possible, gained through direct experience, inner understanding, observation and experimentation. Using the results of those direct experiences, we can then look at ancient texts, and surviving religious/magical taboos to start to piece together a modus operandi for present and future magicians to work with. So let's have a look at how magic and the interactions with consciousness and power can affect the body.

Basic Energy Principles of Magic and the Body

Magical energy works in tides and these tides affect every living thing around them. The effect can alternate between good and bad depending on the action, the magician and the ritual/vision used.

So for example, if a magician or a group of magicians/priests are planning to do a major working, the energy will start to form itself from the moment the time, date and intention is set. The initial action of focussed intent is always the starting point, rather than the beginning of the ritual/visionary work. The magical pattern that is forming from an inner point of view begins to take up power from the egregore of the workers - hence the importance of a magical group having a properly constructed egregore rather than thinking it is some sort of 'group mind'. See my book *The Work of the Hierophant* for details on egregore construction.

As the working date gets closer, the magical inner pattern takes on a more solid form which in turn draws in energy from the inner environment around it: magic needs fuel to work, and where the magical construct gets its power from will ultimately decide how it affects the magicians. Hence the importance of having a specific inner place/temple that the magicians intend to work within during the actual ritual: the inner pattern for the magic begins to build as soon as the inner intent and inner location is decided.

The power continues to build around and within the inner magical pattern which has basically constructed itself. These patterns are complex weaves that will eventually act as filters for a specific magical action and they are the result of angelic and inner contact activity triggered by an external magical intent (the magician) – hence the moral that is repeated in many ancient texts; 'If it is thought, then it is already done'.

How that pattern forms is largely dependant upon the skill of the magician and the strength of the inner contacts around them. It is a balancing act between not interfering too much and not letting it be totally feral: often just a conscious awareness of its existence and keeping that awareness in focus is enough. That focus allows the energy needed to flow to the pattern and also informs the inner beings around the pattern as to your intention so that they can act accordingly.

Energetically imagine this as a seesaw. You the magician is sat on one end and the magical build up/pattern for the event is on the other side. The fulcrum in the middle is usually angelic in the case of ritual/visionary magic. As the event closes in, the need for energy builds. Bear in mind that the energy that flows from you for the event is not just your own energy (unless you do not work with inner beings, inner connections etc), it is joined and mediated through you from the inner worlds, from the inner environment and from the angelic/kabbalistic/deity structure you are working within.

This build up will translate in your life to sensations such as feeling odd, or being sleepy, hungry, or suddenly having to change how you eat, who you talk to etc. As you get very close to the day of work, the energy goes into a slingshot action: the tide of your energy goes far out and then suddenly rebounds in with a bang on the day of working. This has happened to me every time I have done any major working, teaching, consecrating etc... the week before I am very tired as my 'tide has gone out', the day before the work I am useless, but the morning of the work I am fired up with tons of power as the tide comes back in and that power level is maintained until the day after the work. The day after the magical work I will crawl out of bed like an old woman and just want to sleep or watch bad TV.

This is the slingshot and tide effect. The power builds from intent and the opposing side of your seesaw starts to go down; this is experienced as the tide going out. Once it has reached its critical point and it is time for action, there is a sudden release of energy: the tide comes in and you as mediator have that power flowing through you as you work. It is like the load on the opposing side of the seesaw is suddenly knocked off and you are catapulted upwards.

If your body is generally healthy and well looked after, then the power dynamic will not have any negative lasting effect upon your health and wellbeing. If there is any weakness in your body, or slight imbalance, it can highlight that imbalance for you and you will get stronger symptoms for a few days. That is the signal that you need to pay closer attention to your body. If you are power working in this way frequently over a long period of time, and you have any body weakness at all, it really will begin to take its toll upon you. Just as people burn out from too much work or over competing in sports, so the magician can burn out from over working with too much power too frequently. It's about using common sense.

What I have found personally is that if I do not try and control the form of the pattern in the early stages of development, rather I let nature do its magical thing, then the impact is much less. So for example, I set the intention to gather workers together for a day of magical work in service. With the setting of the intention I book a date. Rather than look for an astrologically profound date, I just go with the flow and take a date when everyone and the venue is available. I do not filter who comes: I put out the word and who turns up is welcomed and worked with. The work intent is also kept loose, rather than saying we are going to do a working to affect this outcome or that outcome in a specific way. I approach it as; the inner worlds have expressed a need for magical work to support the land/a disaster/the future, so we will work in service, open the gates, mediate power and work in ritual and vision for whatever is necessary to bring balance to the situation.

We become a link in the chain of beings who are working, and our bodies are supported by the long line of beings involved in the magical action. If however we do a magical working for a specific agenda, and for a specific outcome, then less beings tend to be willing to work that way and the ones that are willing usually want something in return, including a bit of your energy. This way of working does have a longer lasting drain upon your system and you need to take that into account if you wish to work that way.

Simple focussed magical intent at the start of the planning phase triggers a strong inner impulse for a pattern to form. Those patterns, which are lower octaves of fate patterns, will allow the magic to happen and how you handle the magic will decide how that pattern is fuelled, which in turn will decide how your body is impacted.

Power on Full Throttle

Just before the work is about to start, the tide rushes in and the magician/s are filled with power that will enable them to do the job in hand. When handled in a focussed way and used only for the job, the power flows in an easily accessible way and maintains the magician until the work is finished. A side effect of this filling with power is that any physical or spiritual issue that the magician may have, where the body is trying to adjust (as opposed to being sick), will be catalysed. If it is an issue that the magician is aware of and is willing to address, then the power gets behind the issue as a catalyst and helps the process along.

You begin to see what a delicate balancing act this can be. If you are sick and you carry any amount of power in a magical act, then it will ultimately weaken you. If you are not sick, but are trying to get stronger or more balanced, then any action you are taking to address this situation will be helped along. The power always flows through you as a filter first, adjusting and bringing balance before flowing from you into the magical pattern you are working upon.

The feeling of being filled with such power can be heady and easily knock a magician off balance emotionally if they are not fully aware of their emotional or spiritual weaknesses. This is why the oft repeated maxim – 'magician, know thyself' is so very important. If you really know yourself and face yourself in an honest way, when the power triggers an emotive weakness it is immediately recognised, observed and then put to one side to be worked with. The power can make you feel all powerful, all knowing and all 'messiah' like. It can make you feel invincible, full of strength and vitality, but if you know that in reality it is only the power passing through you, it does not knock you out of whack.

However if you are not used to self-examination in the cold light of day, and do not fully accept yourself and your down sides, then the power comes through in an unbalanced way and spins you out as it passes through. This can manifest itself in a number of ways from becoming controlling of the work/knowledge, to a developing sense of evangelism. It can also divert the attention of the magician from the true path of learning, development and evolution through experience so that the magician spends all of their time trying to classify, box and control the system of magic. This is like a trap that the magician becomes caught up in as they try to grab the inherent knowledge within the power.

A healthier way to interact with the knowledge and insights that flow from power is to acknowledge it and then let it go. By flowing through you that knowledge becomes embedded within you and surfaces when needed to work through you. If you take a major power hit and suddenly decide 'you've got it!' and begin to systematise it in great detail, then you know you have taken a hit and it is expressing through the need to control.

It is a fine line between evolving from experience and passing that on, to playing 'lego' with magical knowledge and power. The difference is in your own perceptions, mutability and ability to let it go.

A simple wisdom that also applies to managing the power as it comes through is to just use it for its intended purpose and then let it go, rather than finishing the work and then taking on another physical or emotive task. When we are filled with power we feel physically strong and in simple terms, this can make us lift boxes our muscles would rather we didn't.

It can also fill us with emotions that are not real. This often manifests with sudden hormonal outbursts and people who would not normally match up, leave the magical work and go have wild sex in a hotel. That often leads to very embarrassing and unhealthy situations when the power wears off. So it is important for anyone leading the group of workers to be aware of this and look out for it.

If the couple are still attracted to each other after the magical power has dissipated, then all is good and it is not anything to do with the group leader. But if it flares up straight after working, it is wise to find a polite way to intervene. The simplest way, and the way I handle it, is to go out for coffee with the group after working and let the dust settle. Within a couple of hours the power wears off and common sense returns. As is with all magic – it is not about the morals; it's about the reality of power and taking responsibility for that power.

Release of Power after Work

After the power has worn off and retreated the body and mind slump, leaving the magician drooling in the corner for a while. A normal healthy body takes about two days to recover from a major magical power working. The body will need food, rest, warmth and relaxation. The mind will need quiet, and plenty of mental 'chewing gum' to entertain but not tax the mind. Things start to come back online after a day or two and any weakness that is in the body will make itself known to the magician so it can be dealt with.

If the magician is older, has been ill, or is female and going through hormone changes, it will take longer to recover. Similarly, if the magician has worked powerfully for many years, then the body's coping mechanisms will start to weaken and show signs of struggle: this will manifest as profound and prolonged weakness after the work that can last for months.

This is the sign to the magician that it is time to shift the work method, down grade the power levels worked with, or go into semi-retirement. This is the stage I am at: at the time of writing this I am finding it harder to recover from powerful work, my hormones are changing (I'm fifty) and also the inner contacts are pushing me to work more and more in a scribe and advisor capacity rather than as a visionary worker. That may change in the future or it may not; the wisdom is knowing what is in front of you, dealing with it appropriately and keeping an open mind regarding the future. Such a shift comes after decades of work and is akin to an athlete knowing when to hang the running shoes up and become a coach rather than a runner.

If the magical power levels that are worked with are not high, then these issues become irrelevant. There is much to be said for slow and steady. Many magical groups/lodges train their magicians slowly and never or very rarely work with high levels of power. The up side of that approach is that there is no burn out. The down side is it can ossify the magic and nothing powerful ever really gets done: it becomes a feel good exercise with lots of padding and no content. I guess the real balance is somewhere in the middle. For me, I'm an extreme sports kinda gal so moderation is a word I never really fully understood. I think different people need different approaches and together, we all make a magical whole!

Holding the Reins

When you begin to work with higher levels of power in magic, interesting dynamics kick in to teach you about how power works. Once a magician works with powers beyond a certain level in ritual/ vision it ceases to be an individual act and becomes a collaborative act whereby different orders of beings, various threads of energy and magical patterns all come together to create a 'bridge' for power to pass from un-being into being.

For the magician, learning how to be a part of that collaboration is a major learning curve and although each situation is different, there are basic principles that underpin such work. The first principle that makes itself quickly apparent is the dynamic of 'bridging' rather than control. If the magician tries to over form the filter (ritual) for the power, or tries to control it too much, he limits the amount of power that can be bridged and he takes the full body impact of the power. Why is this?

When you are moving large amounts of power around and you are working collaboratively, you are one of a team: you will be expected to carry what you are able to carry and no more. If you construct/ work with only what filters are absolutely needful, then the magical ritual pattern is not over formed; the inner contacts understand what you are attempting to achieve, and the minimum filtering allows for the bigger picture to manifest. This in turn allows the inner beings to do their jobs without hindrance: everyone pulls their weight and the job gets done.

If the working is over controlled or over filtered with complex ritual, then these dynamics do not manifest. If the ritual is unnecessarily lengthy with lots of flowery wordage, or the vision is over formed and psychologised, or the calling of the contacts done with very specific names that are often subdivisions of bigger beings (e.g. a Key of Solomon working), then the filter constructed is most often too dense. The consciousness of the inner beings cannot flow back and forth through the magical pattern therefore the energetic burden falls upon the magician. This in turn impacts the health and strength of the magician.

On the other end of the spectrum, if the magical work is not formed enough, or is chaotic or 'free-formed' then there is not enough structure for the power to work through. Similarly, working in an ad hoc way without ritual structure, and relevant inner contacts will result in a magical failure. The most the magician will achieve under such conditions is connections with parasitical beings who will manipulate the magician for their own ends. Usually though under such circumstances, nothing of any relevance happens other than a bit of play acting and wishful thinking.

If however the working is balanced, then the magician will be very tired after a hard day's work and may need a day or two to recover if the work was powerful, but they will have no lasting energetic connection to the work, nor any damage from the work.

Remember...magic is hard work!!!!

Heightened Sensitivity

Another body issue of magic is one of heightened sensitivity. This can be really good or really bad, or both. As inner power flows through you, it filters through your body before going off into the magical pattern to do its job. When the body has that amount of energy flowing through it, it will stimulate regeneration and rebalancing. The more that the body is exposed to this passage of power, the more things strengthen up within you as it passes through. The down side of this is that it can 'over pump' your immune system so that you begin to react to things in your environment that are inherently imbalanced or unhealthy.

So for example, it is not unusual to find adepts who have developed allergies to things in their environment that are toxic: the body is kicked into action when it comes into contact with something that is unbalanced. For example, I became allergic to plastic. Great. No long conversations on the phone for me! I observed this over and over again in long term working adepts who were bringing through power: while their essential organs and structure were youthful for their age and very strong, they would have allergic reactions to a lot of things.

It does seem that the longer adepts work with inner power at depth, the more tuned into their environment they become, and the more psychic they become. So although the body of the adept sometimes takes hits from over work, or doing heavy inner work and from grappling with beings, (or making stupid mistakes like me) the underlying structure of the body, in general, is strong and regenerative. The deeper connection to the environment/land however will cause the magician to react to anything toxic or unhealthy.

You can assist this development of sensitivity to make it work for you rather than against you. In my twenties, my then teacher would send me off to junk shops and charity shops to handle old things to see how they felt. At that time, I could feel some things, but it was faint. It took some time for me to become aware of the 'clogged energy' that was left on my hands from handling various discarded belongings. I kept up the exercise, and still do to this day, of handling things to get a 'feel' of where they had been, what had been done with them etc.

My sensitivity jumped up many notches when I began working deeper in the inner realms and these days, there are things I just cannot bear to handle, as they feel so disgusting. That sensitivity also expresses not just in your hands, but in how you see and feel, how you smell things and how you sense things. It creeps up on you gradually as your body becomes more and more attuned to power, energy and spirit. Therefore it is important that you learn to listen to your senses and what your body is trying to tell you: it is as if the deeper work brings long forgotten skills out of our DNA and wakes it back up.

It is important when developing this process to not second guess, analyse or try to control this developing sensitivity. Just let it develop in its own way and there will come a day when you really feel it in action and it saves your ass.

The physical sensitivities that manifest as allergies in some magicians are the body's way of telling you that you are exposing yourself to something that is toxic, counter productive to your work or health. So again, listen to the body and just go with it.

An interesting one that manifests a lot for magicians is a perfume allergy. It took me a while to realise that a lot of our most subtle endocrine functions centre around scents and smells. How we unconsciously communicate with other people and the world around us through smell, how we read people, how we interact with beings, are alerted to danger, particularly in a magical context comes through the sense of smell. If we douse ourselves in chemical smells, or are surrounded in our homes by chemical smells, then we cannot access these subtle senses. The body, primed by magical power, recognises these chemicals as potential threats to our wellbeing and reacts accordingly.

Magic will change your body and working sensibly with those tides and changes will help you to strengthen in the face of heavy work. Magic takes its toll in terms of hard work, but it also provides the energetic nourishment and strength to maintain magical power if it is done properly. Just don't push your luck!!

Knowing Your Body

Having an understanding of your body, how it works and what its weaknesses are, form a major part of magical understanding. Your body is the filter than magic passes through, so that filter must be properly maintained. Each body is different and that is an important point to think about; when your body becomes a magical filter, the power causes changes to your body which in turn changes how your body reacts to stimulus, food and sickness.

As you progress in magic, you may notice that one particular organ takes the strain; that is an early warning sign that the method you are using to bring the power through is imbalanced. It took me many years to work that detail out, not only for myself but for other magicians around me. For me it was my uterus and it is a common reactive organ in women when they are working with power. The uterus brings life into the world and as such is built to house a new life, energy and consciousness.

For myself it manifested as pain, irregular bleeding when doing heavy magic and eventually uterine disorders. It took a long time for me to work out that the method of magic I was using was unbalanced: I worked almost exclusively in vision with very little externalised ritual. I am a natural visionary, so rather than learning early on to balance such use of vision with exteriorised patterns in the form of ritual expression, I played to my strengths when I should have attended to my weaknesses.

It took many years of working with other magicians for me to realise that power needs an externalised pattern to manifest through, otherwise it will manifest powerfully through your own body.

I used to keep magical diaries that plotted out what I was doing, and what magical results I was having, but it did not occur to me for a long time to also keep a record of body reactions. If I had, I would have picked up on the dynamic much sooner. But I did slowly begin to realise that powerful work that was not anchored properly affected people's minds and bodies in a variety of ways. Once I understood that dynamic I paid more attention, kept tighter records and adjusted my working methods accordingly.

Many of the older magical texts used by magicians have religious dogmas and cultural taboos woven into the magical system and many are simply irrational dogmas that have developed through the medieval mindset. Our challenge in today's magical world is to differentiate between what elements of the magical text are proper filters, contacts etc, and what is useless baggage that clogs up the filters. What taboos are there to protect the body and soul of the magician and what is simple window dressing? We are at a stage of magical development that calls for revisiting some of these archaic mindsets and re-evaluating them. It needs to come from individual observations, personal direct experiences and the observations of others. That way we truly move forward in our understanding and are better able to discern what is wisdom and what is superstition. That cannot come from theoretical analysis, but by experimentation with an open mind.

I think the way forward, in body/mind maintenance of the magician, particularly if you are forging your own path or are embarking on exploration, is simply to listen to your body and take nothing at face value. Challenge rules to find out by direct experience why they are there.

Symptoms and Empathy

Another observation on the subject of magic and the body I made over the years, and one that has fascinated me beyond description is the reality of body symptoms. What do I mean by that? In the world of medicine and biological sciences, when the body manifests symptoms of disease, it is the direct result, or the body's reaction to an illness, infection or malfunction. Simple. Or so I thought.

Quite early on in magic I began to notice something curious happening in two very distinct areas of magic. One was healing and the other was high powered workings. The dynamic in healing is something that is well reported even if not fully understood, and that is the dynamic whereby a healer takes on the symptoms of the sick person and processes them, relieving the burden of the sick person.

The second dynamic is whereby symptoms, be they acute or chronic in a magician are temporarily transferred to another person when it is imperative that the magician undertakes a major magical working that must be completed.

I had been aware from being quite young that if I was stood next to a sick person, I could 'feel' their illness and I would sometimes manifest the symptoms without intention. The sick person would feel much better and I would become sick. Usually the sickness would not last long in me and would dissipate quickly. I also found from being young that if someone was very ill, even if they did not know it, I would get very drained and ill just being in the same room with them, whereas they would have a temporary reprieve and feel great. For years I concluded this was just an energy drain, and sometimes it is just that.

But then I began to notice my body taking on their symptoms while their symptoms reduced – much more than simply energy deficits. For example: I was working with a fellow magician who had high blood pressure and was on various medications, many of which were not really working very well. He asked me to work on him and I agreed. He had a blood pressure gauge with him so I decided to experiment. He took his blood pressure, which was very high and then took mine, which is naturally low.

After I had worked on him, I immediately got a terrible headache and felt horrible. He took his blood pressure which had dropped significantly and then took mine which was through the roof! I had never had high blood pressure! His blood pressure stayed stable for months and mine dropped back to normal within hours but it was a revelation that got me thinking. Was the healing work the cause of the spike in my blood pressure or did I take on his symptoms?

Over the next year or so I talked to a few different healers who had trained in various traditions and they reported similar dynamics but their traditions had methods for working with that dynamic to protect the healer. Eventually a good friend of mine took me to one side and suggested I would be bad material for a healer. Not because I could not heal, but because my natural ability was too feral; this could make it dangerous for me. Unless I was willing to focus all of my attention on proper training for a prolonged period of time, it would be counter productive for me. I took the advice on board and stopped doing hands on healing for people. I did eventually spend time studying homeopathy and cranial osteopathy, mainly for use on my children and magical colleagues, but even then I became too exposed to people's symptoms and never really learned how to shut that down.

The second dynamic (remember that one?) regarding the shifting of symptoms from one person to the next is something that I could find little about but observed a lot in magical practice. This happens when the magician has an illness or disease and has symptoms. The magician also has been called to take on a magical job but the symptoms would hinder the work of the magician. So the person closest to the magician manifests the symptoms, the magician becomes symptom free and the job gets done. After the job is finished the magician gets the symptoms back and the carrier goes back to normal. Outlandish? Yes. True? Oh yes, this has happened to me more times that I care to think about, and in both directions.

Handing Over Your Symptoms

Like many things in my life, this had to happen a few times before I became aware of the dynamic. I had noticed before that no matter how tired or pre menstrual or sick I was, if there was heavy magical work to be done, a rush of power came in and I felt great (remember the tides discussed earlier?).

It took a bit longer for me to notice that when I was magically needed to be on top form and my symptoms vanished; someone else close to me got them. This was different from load sharing, which happens a lot in my family, whereby the deficit of energy caused by a major event would be shared out between family members.

The passing back and forth of symptoms, for me, was only noticed when I got into my forties. It coincided with a chronic illness that took hold of me in my mid forties and that stayed with me for 5 years. During that time, I did less magic and more writing but when I was called upon to do necessary magical work I would feel great and be symptom free whereas my partner would have my symptoms. As soon as the magical work was over, my partner would feel better and my symptoms would come back. Fascinating!

It was not something that was conscious or that I had tried to do, it would just happen. And this is another example of how power works when you do not try to control the magic too much: the inner tides work with you and facilitate whatever is needful to get the job done. I asked my partner if he wanted me to find a way to block it and he said no: it was his contribution to the work. And this is one of the dynamics that plays out in a magical group or lodge: the group works as a hive energy with burdens passing back and forth as needed to ensure a job is done. It all balances out in the end so that no one person is left holding the can.

But a deeper question that comes up from this observation is what truly is illness then? If very visible and obvious physical symptoms can be switched on and off or moved from one body to another, then they are not what we think they are. From observing my own body through illness and also keeping a close eye on others, the only conclusion I could come to is that body symptoms are a vocabulary rooted in an energy/power deficit. Fill the deficit and the body reactions go away, move the deficit from one person to another and the symptoms move accordingly.

Which brings me to another train of thought. If it was just a matter of energy deficit, then surely when power is taken from one body and given to another, the body in deficit would show symptoms specific to the weaknesses in that specific body. But it does not happen that way. The symptoms that manifest are moved intact from one body to another and mirrored exactly in the other person. Is there some being, pattern or consciousness that elicits particular reactions in bodies? So it would be similar in some ways to the action of something like a virus (which we also cannot see). A specific virus creates a series of reactions in a body that identifies that virus: for example the chickenpox virus will cause a distinct rash.

Is this what we are looking at? That many of these unidentifiable chronic illnesses are caused by a being or pattern that sucks energy out of the body in a specific way therefore causing specific symptoms? Hence if you fill the energy deficit the body replenishes itself temporarily and the person donating the energy holds the 'pattern or consciousness' for a short while. If that were the case then would not that donor also become infected? But that does not seem to happen.

Or is it that we are seeing a magician unconsciously holding a thread of a vast magical pattern (remember when you asked to be of service? Ha! You will learn to keep your mouth shut!!). Could that magical pattern trigger certain responses and energy deficits within the body that become symptoms when the body's energy becomes low? I think this is the more likely scenario. And it is also something I have come across within religious patterns.

What has all this to do with magic you ask? Everything. How we work, how our energy responds, how beings operate around us, how we can unconsciously be working on a long term project and not realise, how we maintain our bodies as power filters are all a part and parcel of powerful magic.

This unconscious working of long term patterns is interesting. The first aspect of this goes back, for me, to the heady days in my 30s where I undertook some massive magical projects. I assumed when I had finished my part of the work that my energetic involvement with the project was over. Twenty years later I realise that I only walked away from the outer manifestation of that work and that the power is still flowing, still unfolding. I am inexorably linked to that process at a deep level: the work is ongoing and at some level my energy is still working on it. (Hence be careful what you agree to magically.)

Effects of Exploration

Not every magician/priestess wishes to explore or push boundaries within the inner or outer worlds of power and magic, but some do. Many are not capable, not because they are useless, but because their skill set is in a different area. I can find things, hack into things, gain access to inner places and communicate with random beings. Not all magicians can do that, but then there are many things that other magicians can do easily that I have to work very hard to achieve. It is about working with your strengths while also building up your weaknesses.

I am a 'curious cat': I need to know why, how, where, whom etc. I have never taken things at face value, or accepted other people's word; I need to know for my self and to have direct experience. On the plus side that has driven me for decades in the inner worlds, constantly pushing boundaries, experimenting and going where any sane person would fear to tread.

On the down side, as with all forms of exploration, you hit barriers, trigger guardians, fall down holes, get stuck in places and meet very large beings who want to eat you. I have always thrived on this kind of challenge; as a late teen I did a lot of potholing/caving, pushing my physical and emotional limits and vanishing into tight dark holes in search of what was around the corner. This mentality stayed with me into adulthood and has been a major theme of my magical practice.

Such exploration brings new understanding, a broader view and allows us to break through into deeper and more obscure magical places and conditions. I would say that 90% of what I have learned in magic over the decades has come from exploratory work, with my findings been translated into understandings by looking over the results in context of ancient texts, teachers feedback etc. The thrill of finding something obscure and odd, only to have it confirmed in some ancient writing or by an elder who says, "ah yes, I know what that is... it is blah..." Knowing that you are on the right track, are stepping through the mysteries and finding all the staging posts is a wonderful exciting feeling.

It does have a major downside though and that is the body effect. If I had known about this before hand, I would still have explored, but would have looked after my body better and would have made a point of reaching for inner contacts to help teach me about how to handle my body through this work. Hence this part of the chapter.

When you reach into an inner place that has not had human contact for a very long time, you often come across what is experienced as an energetic membrane that slowly grows across the inner place that is no longer in regular use. Another way to describe it is as a build up of obstruction, or a slow sealing of a place energetically. When an inner place or temple or realm is in more or less constant use by magicians, priestesses etc, a path is formed that makes it easier for our consciousness to travel. When the place has not been used, that path dies away and the explorer has to hack through the obstruction to break back into a space. This takes a lot of energy and while you do not always feel it while you are working, you most certainly do a few hours afterwards. That impact is akin to digging through a rock slide underground: you are exhausted afterwards and your muscles ache.

The same dynamic of energy plays out when you meet an inner being/contact for the first time and the being has not had human contact either before, or for a very long time. The energetic effort to bridge consciousness to that being is very hard and really can knock the stuffing out of you. Sometimes, if that contact or place is due to be released or opened back out into the world, then it is like popping a boil, it's easy, there is no pressure and feels like you have done nothing. That is because there is so much energetic build up for the action, and you are just playing your part in a bigger picture.

Sometimes when you reach deep into the inner worlds for a very ancient contact, or one that does not usually work with humanity anymore, the energy of the bridging to that contact gives you a bit of a stuffing. The contact itself, i.e. the power frequency of the contact or place can in itself have a massive impact upon your body as it is a power we are not really built to interact with. So sometimes deep contacts can adversely affect you without meaning to, just by the frequency of their power; it's like radiation poisoning.

Many years ago, I was working with a group of magicians and we were reaching far back in time for ancient contacts upon the land. Being young and stupid, I wanted to see just how far back I could go. I did manage to reach way back into the consciousness of the land and made contact with a being that was so different from me that we could not find a way to communicate. We just hung out in each others space briefly, tried various forms of contact communication and eventually gave up. Afterwards I felt very weird. Two hours later my partner and I felt really weird, disorientated, nauseous and weak. It lasted for days and really knocked the stuffing out of me.

So how could that affect have been avoided? The impact of deep work cannot ever be completely sidestepped as it comes with the territory, but there are ways to support the body, build up to it and re balance it afterwards. It never occurred to me in those days that the body needs to learn how to build 'inner muscle', to learn to slowly adapt, strengthen etc; I would just dive in. That is equivalent to trying to climb a high rock face with no training, no muscle development and no tools; your arms and shoulders will hurt like shit afterwards and you may get injuries, if you didn't fall to your death that is. Let's look at how that can be avoided and how we can strengthen and prepare for deep exploration.

Body Matters

The way to prepare your body and build stamina is best done through staging your work and learning to walk before you can run. People with natural talent for working with magic may feel able to dive in and experiment straight away, and they can make magic work powerfully, but it often eventually ends in a burn out or crash. It is worth building a solid foundation for the body to work with so that the work continues over a longer period of time.

Learning to still the mind and learning how to establish an outer ritual pattern that will then connect with inner vision anchors the work and takes some of the impact off the body in the early days. This can be achieved by working within a ritual space with an altar or altars, first reaching for an inner contact via the outer thresholds at the altars and then building up the ritual pattern in both an outer and inner sense.

The method I used was four directional altars and an altar in the centre. I would have people first learn how to light the inner and outer candle in each direction, and then progress to calling in inner contacts to the threshold of the altars from four distinct lines of power that were anchored at each altar. This first stage of working is discussed at length in my book *Magical Knowledge I*.

Once that (or any other) basic pattern of ritual and contact is established and has been worked with for a while, it is time to begin learning and working in the inner worlds through well-known and well-established inner patterns, the Great Library, for example. Learning how to work in the Inner Desert, the Great Library, Death, the Underworld, the Stars, the Inner Temples etc not only allows you to exercise your inner muscles and gets them strong, it also teaches you about how the different types of inner contact work, what effect they have on you, what their limitations are and what they are willing and able to do in terms of your work and theirs.

When those basics are all fully established, you have a much stronger set of skills to then begin to explore less trodden paths and open new ones. If you are reaching for a deep or ancient contact, then it is wise to attempt the connection in stages: do not reach right back as a first action, but attempt a series of steps back so that you approach the deepest contact by way of stages and other intermediary contacts.

Once you have broken through into a new/deep contact, the trick to lessen the impact on your body is to externalise the contact through ritual, image building (a deity image for example) and learn to work with them in vision but at the threshold of your space. After a while you will learn through action and experiment how to completely externalise the contact and power you have connected with and this step, of all of them, grounds the power and stops it backing up in your body.

So for example if you have been exploring and working with a very ancient deity/Titan in vision, then you need to externalise that bridging. That can be done by going out on the land that is connected to them or compatible with them. Stand upon the land and talk to them using your physical voice; sit on the land, commune with them and be aware of them. This action balances the extreme inner contact; it balances the energy scales.

The next step would be to work in your magical space. Light a candle in the working direction and call them with your voice and also using vision, to the threshold of the altar. This is the beginning of the bridging. By this time you will have also formed an idea of what they look like to you. Don't let your imagination dress them up (yellow robe, pink hat, sparkly eyes etc), just focus on the key elements that they present to you. It does not matter if it is not a whole picture as that will develop over time. This will enable you to create an externalised image or statue that can then become the focus of work.

Because you have already connected with them in the inner worlds and then brought them to the threshold in ritual, they are able to cross the threshold into our world, externalising their power without any further need of inner action from us.

By externalising the contact in this way, it grounds it so that it flows through you rather than stays within you. This took me a long time to learn and for a while I was carrying around the burden of many contacts within me which was like having a 50lb weight strapped to my back. When I felt I could not carry this weight anymore, I finally listened to my old teacher when she said if you need to learn something, go to the library. So I did.

I went in vision a few times to the Great Library and said I needed to learn how to process these burdens of contact as it was trashing my body. The knowledge was put within me (this often shows as the inner contact pushing a book into your body) and unfolded slowly over a couple of years. The only way I can describe it is to say it was like having an invisible friend walking along side me and patiently guiding my actions, nudging me, inspiring me to go somewhere only to find myself stood out in nature wondering what the hell to do next.

It was at a visit to the ocean one day when I finally got it. I had been working and exploring at great depth something called the Sea Temple, which is a series of contacts and deep 'temples' out at sea from the very distant past. It was a strong inner contact and I worked in vision with these contacts for a long while but the burden was beginning to takes its toll.

I stood on the edge of the sea and dropped a drop of my blood into the ocean to let the contacts know who I was and who my ancestors where. I stood with my feet in the sea, just on the edge, and used my voice to acknowledge them and welcome them back to communion with humanity. It was that simple. I didn't feel anything happening and I thought I had failed. I went home and promptly fell into a long and very deep sleep.

The following day I woke up very groggy, but within a couple of hours I felt amazing: the burdens had gone, the contact had bridged full circle from outer element, to inner worlds and back to outer element. I went back to the ocean and got an immediate response from the sea and the wind; I could talk to the contact in its deity/ inner contact form, but it was grounded in nature therefore in its full power and not being carried around by me. I visited the sea regularly from that point on until we moved inland. I would go and verbally talk to the sea, tell the sea what I was trying to learn or do, and then I would sit down in vision and connect with the inner contact either deep in the Sea Temple or on the seashore.

The bridging into nature of an ancient contact not only took the burden off me, but also allowed me to learn about the dynamics of power in nature and thus helped me learn about working and protecting my own body.

Elements and Contacts within the Human Body

An important and often overlooked part of magic and the human body is the sense of connection with the different consciousness that make up the human body. It is easy to forget that the body is merely a vehicle for us and that the body is essentially a hive being.

The human body is full of different bacteria, viruses etc all of which have their own consciousness from a magical point of view. Beyond that there is the ancient concept that key organs also have their own consciousness that can be communed with.

I came across this purely by accident when a healer pointed out to me that I needed to talk to my organs. I had developed a method of talking to my endocrine system by imagining my adrenals, for example, as hard working mice on a treadmill, keeping an eye out in all directions for any potential threat. This allowed my mind to influence the performance of the adrenals and I worked with the same method on my thyroid, hypothalamus etc. I found I was able to 'nudge' the action of these glands by using thought and interaction. But I had never talked to an organ. I was sceptical.

I tried it, starting first with my heart and I was shocked by the result: I did not need to form a visionary/imagined interface as a consciousness was there already, in full form, appearing as a king. I began working with him and eventually came to the understanding that certain key organs did indeed have their own form of 'consciousness' and together they made up a collective that my spirit could operate through. I tried to get my head around this magically, biologically and spiritually, but I eventually gave up and just went with the flow. Hey, it worked, and at the end of the day that was all that mattered.

Over time I began to see correlations between these key organs and spheres of the Tree of Life (heart/king/solar/ Tiphereth)..duh....and began to realise that some of the body connections with the Tree of Life were not just the result of men wanting to make lists, put power in boxes and find connections where there were none.

I went into the Great Library and asked for learning on this subject and slowly that learning began to filter out into my outer life. It is still unravelling and I am still in the learning process, so there is little detail I can give of findings other to say, look at this, find out for yourself; it is fascinating and also very useful.

An interesting way the knowledge that I requested in the Great Library exteriorised was via a book that came my way. This is often the way it happens with the Great Library: you ask for learning and in response you are first put through certain circumstances, and then appropriate books or people are put in your path so that you can study. The book appeared just at the right time, as I had by then developed a way of talking to the organs; what I then needed was more solid information so that I did not have to re invent the wheel.

The book was about the Classical Five Elements and Guardians system of acupuncture. I nearly did not get the hint but something made me stop and buy the book. It was all about what I had been experiencing: the consciousness of organs, the interface between spirit and body and how they all work together to keep the body and soul together in harmony. Although the Chinese element system is different to a Western Magical System (we do not work with wood as an element for example), the basic concepts and mechanisms are the same and the principles of the system work. Fascinating! I am at the stage where I am still reading, learning, experiencing and hopefully I will be able to be more coherent around the subject in years to come.

What it did confirm for me is something which I have worked with for a while with magic and the body is the need to balance the elements out within magical practice. Working with too much fire for example will put a strain on your kidneys/water system as the body tries to compensate for the overload of one element. Although the magical fire is not physical, it does trigger a physical reaction within the body thus creating an imbalance. So be aware of that potential when you work with the elemental directions and powers: keep the inner elements balanced so that the body does not take the strain and have to try and rebalance the elements physically. If you work in depth in one direction and with one element, balance the work by also being active with the other three elements.

Summary

There are more mundane practical aspects of helping your body cope with the impact of heavy magic and the basic rules are: if you are on strong medication or recreational drugs, then do not do heavy/deep inner work. Some medicines/substances will help support the body but in general stronger drugs will make you more vulnerable. It is particularly the case with drugs that affect your endocrine system, serotonin/dopamine/adrenaline levels. There are no hard fast rules, as each body is different, so it pays to listen to your body and act accordingly.

If you are on antibiotics for an infection, then doing exploratory work down the Abyss is probably not the best idea. The Abyss is a fascinating but dangerous place and the deeper you go down it the more dangerous it gets. If your body is already fighting an infection, it cannot also fight off the energetic intrusions that some of the beings can inflict upon your spirit and body. You need to be fit and healthy and of sound mind to explore and work in such depths.

The other rule of thumb is if you are doing a lot of work down the Abyss, or the Underworld or in death, then you need to balance that work by working in the inner temples, working with angelic beings at the edge of the Abyss as they weave the future, or work out in the stars. It is also very important if you are doing deep inner work to get out in nature as much as possible. It can be as simple as standing in a garden, or standing in sunlight, or sitting under a tree; the deeper you work, the more nature responds to you. Make sure you keep your work balanced and your body will then be able to adjust and settle itself.

Working as a magician, unless you are very dense, you are going at some point in time to experience a physical reaction to a being, a place, a building or a magical working. If you are very sensitive, you may possibly experience quite severe reactions to your environment or magical actions.

The key to managing and working productively with this dynamic is know your body, know your environment, know what powers and beings it is that you are working with and act accordingly. If you listen to your body and observe its responses, you will learn how you as an individual handles power. If you learn how to support your body while doing powerful work then you will develop strength and endurance. It's all about using your common sense, respecting life and not thinking that anything magical is going to kiss your life with pink happiness and fluffy love.

Think about the outer equivalent of your work and how that would affect your body. If you are working on building inner temples or repairing them, imagine what your body is going to feel like at the end of the day if you were working outside as a brick layer. Your muscles would hurt and you would be tired. Same rules apply. Remember, inner work affects the outer body, just as outer work affects your inner spirit.

2

Living Magically –
Home/Temple

Chaos behind locked doors

There comes a time in a magical life when you cease 'going' to a temple/lodge/workshop to do magic and instead, you live within the magic. That is a major and an essential step in the development of the magician: the integration of magic in to your life. Through books, media and history, we perceive magic as something that happens away from our ordinary lives, something that is glamorous, something that happens in secret, in groups and behind locked doors. And there is a point and truth to that for many obvious reasons.

But there is also a way to live with magic, to have it be a part of everyday life, and also part of family life. Of course, in some countries and communities there are going to be issues of persecution and potential danger with openly practicing magic and we will look into some aspects of how to be magical at home but in stealth mode. But in general the approach to living magically is with the assumption that you live in a country where you are not going to get arrested and burned at the stake for being a magician!

I have to say that living magically in rural England in the early 90s with two young children was very hard work. I was threatened a couple of times by local church reverends, that I would have my children taken from me. At that time in the UK it was a serious threat.

It was one of the major driving forces behind moving the family to the States for a few years. So I do know only too well how hard it can be to live your own path in public.

Temple v Home

The idea of having a temple/lodge building away from where you live, a place that you only visit a few times a year to do magic is a strange and relatively modern concept. In times past, a magician was also a priest/priestess and worked day after day in the temple, keeping the powers balanced, keeping the long term projects going etc. Even in tribal society, their magic is lived with all the time.

Why would you live around magic all the time? Once you are stepping towards the work of an adept, you will find that you are working magically all the time: you are never 'switched off'. If you are living in a contacted and magically supported environment, then you will cope well with being on magical call 24/7. If however you live in the centre of a city, in a non magical environment and you are carrying a long term magical burden, then you will eventually start to really feel the strain.

People in the occult world often 'dress up' their home as part of their identity. So for example a follower of witchcraft will have brooms, skulls, herbs, pentacles, a nicely displayed altar etc. Self-expression and expression of identity is one thing, a magically operating home is another; it is crucially important to know the difference. If someone came to our home, they would not think it was an 'occult' home, but they may think we were eccentric collectors. You can have a magically operating house that does not really appear to be anything except a little odd. So let's have a look at a magical home, what is in it, how to balance it.

Protection

People immediately think about sealing their homes magically and frantically do the LBRP (lesser banishing ritual of the pentagram) on a regular basis. This is totally unnecessary and will end up defeating the whole sense of magic and protection in the house. I have talked about this at length in other books, but a basic summary is if you are balancing the house with spirits, beings, deities etc, the frequency of the house filters out unnecessary and unwelcome guests that cause problems. It also allows for various beings to come and go in the upkeep of the Work and to reach you when they are in need of help.

Instead of ritual patterns (such as LBRP), in a magical home, guardians guard the threshold, trap unwanted low level beings and keep them busy; the general frequency of the house repels unwanted magic, the use of incense, music and the layout of deities in the house keeps out parasites and other annoying low level beings. The interactions between various compatible deities set up a pattern of energy in the house and the daily brief work with them keeps it all tuned in. The use of specific sigils in vulnerable spots creates a filter/barrier and most importantly of all your interaction on a daily basis with the beings, ancestors and powers that flow through the land where you live together creates a living environment that is dynamic, accessible and relatively safe.

I say relatively safe because this method will not keep everything out, and a magician should never live in a magically sealed environment: it is akin to living in a bacterially sterile environment and fatally weakens the magician. The use of a totally protected space is only really needed when the magician is very sick and even then I would question the wisdom of this. Keeping the house balanced and at a suitable magical frequency allows beings that work within that frequency to come forward to help you, warn you, guard you, teach you or seek you out for help. If a house is sealed with banishing rituals, that casual interaction cannot happen and the magician is left to her own devices.

A magician who lives in a banished and sealed space will find they cannot cope with powerful inner contacts, they are knocked easily when visiting powerful places and they are not able to sustain constant daily casual inner contact. Through modern teaching and popular magical trends, magical students are constantly over protecting themselves and the net result is generations of weak un-contacted or faintly contacted magicians.

If however you work through the methods of frequencies and beings in your home and around you, you may very well take a hit now and again, but what gets through to you is a small percentage of the danger, just enough for you to deal with, learn from and emerge stronger from. Like an immune system, it needs colds and bugs to keep it healthy.

There is also a deeper dynamic of human consciousness playing out through this issue and that is one of ego. A magician who feels he is protected and balanced by using banishing rituals is an idiot. It is the lone boy with his finger in the dam. Magical power and the beings that flow through that power are vast in some circumstances and will break through a banishing ritual in seconds. However if you are living in an environment that is populated by spirits, ancestors and deities, you are a small part of a wider family most of whom are able to deal far better with incoming fire or random beings. You do your part as a physical magician and they do theirs.

You are never totally protected from everything that could be disruptive, but things that you cannot handle are dealt with and things that would teach you are allowed through. If you are over protected you never really learn to deal with the various 'hexes', attacks, parasites, ghosts etc that are all part and parcel of strengthening the magician and keeping you on your toes. But anything that would seriously harm you or interfere with the work is kept at arms length.

Over protection is akin to having angels sweep all humans off the road while you walk down it. So you never learn basic skills such as how to identify someone who is a potential problem or threat, how to identify someone who is in need of help, how to make new friends, how to bump into old friends unexpectedly etc. The skills you use in everyday life are mirrored in magic.

Building a balanced filter in a home takes time, patience and a willingness to learn on the job. There are tons of books out there on magic but at the end of the day we are all still very much back into the magical dark age and we have to relearn so many skills. The only way to do that is to learn what others have discovered but also discover for yourself by 'doing'.

House Deity

The first step to working a house magically is to establish deities or a deity to work with. The relationship is not one of religious worship; rather it is one of deep respect, honour and responsibility. It is your responsibility to build a relationship with the deity, to ensure they have the offerings they need, the candles, scents, gifts and conversations that deities thrive upon. They become honoured members of your family.

Once that power is up and running in the house it creates bedrock for everything else to sit on. The choice of deity to work with is important and should be either a deity who has made themselves known to you repeatedly, or a deity that you have a deep resonance with. Do not choose a deity from the current occult fashion trend, nor is it wise to choose a modern synthetic deity like Baphomet or Babalon. To work well with you and for you to learn magic in depth, you need a deity who is ancient, stable and compatible with the land around you. Some deities are very specific to a culture or a landmass and others have a much wider reach. Some are compatible with magic and family, and some are not.

It is worth taking the time, if a deity or a small group of deities make themselves apparent to you, to find out about them and find out if their power has been subdivided in antiquity, or if they still have opposing powers flowing through them. Ancient powers will have a destructive and creative side to them. Subdivided powers, where the deity has ritually been fragmented into two, will bring a more unbalanced power to the house.

The deity that was the foundation for my home made herself known in my early 20s and people kept giving me gifts of her picture, or statues etc. It took me a while to figure out that she wanted me to work with her. She is an ancient power and has both creative and destructive sides to her, which is a perfect balance.

Once you are sure that it is the right deity for you and your family/home then you need to create a window for that deity to reach through. Just getting a picture or a statue is not enough: that image has to be enlivened for it to work in our world. This enables the power of the deity to flow back and forth into the space and to interact with you. The statue is not the deity itself; it is merely a window that acts as a communication/access point.

There are a variety of ways enlivening can be done and I have discussed various methods in my other books. One way, which I have not discussed previously, is to take a direct transmission and transplant it into the statue at home. This only works with a limited amount of deities simply because there are only a small number of enlivened deities still functioning and accessible to us. The action itself can be a major learning curve as it needs a variety of skills and abilities to do it, as well as access to an enlivened deity.

The first step is finding a statue of your chosen deity that is enlivened and still operative. It is worth bearing in mind that by the Roman/Greek classical era, the skills to enliven a deity were fragmenting and ebbing away. The same is true now of many Indian deities; the statues are no longer enlivened, rather they are 'blessed' which is something different. So it is worth trying to reach for a deity statue from ancient Egypt, or pre British India, or early Greek/Roman/ Etruscan, etc.

Old deities that are full of power but where there is little knowledge about them is a bit more risky. For example, Belinos, a solar deity from pre Roman Britain is much used within Wiccan circles, but as a power we know little about this deity and the power he brought through. A whole modern construct of revival paganism has created a mythos to work with him and that work is used within a 'worship' context. Now that's fine in such a setting and the fact that no one actually knows what is coming through that deity pattern is also ok; the relationship is still arms length and is not a working relationship. However if that deity was brought into a magical household and worked with in great depth, it might be a different matter.

Belinos has not been consistently worked with as an active deity and the revival of the last 100 years is a simple drop in the ocean in deity terms. So that power could be unstable, could be parasited, it could be a destructive deity, there is no way of telling and because there has been such a break in 'work' (not worship) with this power, it is a major risk using such a power as a foundation for magical work in a home setting. So unless you are a total bomb-head adventurer with no kids in the house, stick with the powers that have had a lot of work done with them, are stable and can be easily identified.

Once you have chosen your deity, then you need to find a source for direct transmission. This could be a museum, a temple at home or abroad, or a private collection. What you need is a statue that was at one point in a working temple, a statue that has been ritually enlivened and is still functional. You will be able to tell which ones are enlivened and which ones are not, but it does take patience and practice.

When trying to find the enlivened statue (and not every statue in a museum is enlivened) the first step is to go very still internally, which is not easy in a busy museum. Find a place to sit, be still, and work with a void/stillness meditation with your eyes open. Once you are still and tuned in, begin to walk around the statues that you are trying to connect with. Some will feel like nothing, some you will feel a resistance to, like a field of energy around them, and some may jump out at you by talking to you, or appearing in your inner vision.

The ones that reach out in communication or make themselves very apparent are the ones that are enlivened. The ones with the feeling of energy around them are not fully enlivened, but they are tuned. If a deity really makes themselves known, remember that the last time they were properly talked to was probably in a temple by priests and priestesses who worshipped them as well as worked magically with them. They will expect to be honoured, they will expect to be respected and that is how it should be: blind worship of deities by priests came towards the end of the life cycle of the temple. Every temple has a life span and when the priesthood degenerates from balanced respect and magical interaction to blind worship you have the end of a true temple. Honour them by acknowledging them in your mind and then find a place very near them where you can sit.

Close your eyes and work in vision. Go in vision and stand or kneel before the deity. Tell them who you are, what you do and what you are trying to achieve. Ask if they wish to come home with you to live in a sanctuary there and be worked with. If they agree then it is time to do the transmission. If they refuse, ask them if there is anything you can do for them and if it is something you can do, then do it. They may come home with you another time; it is not something you can force.

When the deity agrees, open your eyes and go to stand by them. It is important that the transmission is physical: only a small amount of people are capable of taking on the burden of deity without touch, so it is important to make physical contact with the statue. This can get you into a lot of trouble as most museums freak out if you touch the statues. But if the place is busy or the guard is distracted, just look as if you are trying to see something close up on the statue or down the side of it. As you get close, ask the deity in your mind and utter it under your breath for them to come into you, to reside within you until you can transfer them into a statue. By asking, you give permission for the deity to pass into you; if you don't ask, it will not happen.

The actual physical contact does not need to take long; a brief touch is often enough - make sure your hands are clean and have no oil or any other residue; it is also important to protect the physical integrity of an ancient artefact. When I did it for the deity I work with, I briefly touched her feet while pretending to tie my shoelace. It was enough. I had asked her to come into me, she had announced she wanted to be working with me; it all came together swiftly and powerfully.

Bear in mind what is passed into you is not the deity in its entirety; it is more like a 'signature' or even the idea of a GPS so that the power that is that deity can access you through a frequency that you then place in the statue at home.

It can be difficult for us to get our heads around such an idea as a deity transfer as we are used to being single units. The idea that a deity power can flow through multiple units at once can be difficult for some to understand. So think of a statue as a plugged in telephone. The transmission into you is the telephone number which you take home and 'program' into the statue.

Carrying the transmission can be a bit of a burden on the body. When I have carried such transmissions, I want to eat like a horse, sleep like the dead and it makes me feel very weak and tired. The reason for this is it takes a lot of energy to carry such a transmission so the sooner you can transfer it to a statue the better.

Transferring the Transmission into the Statue

This part of the work is fairly simple but you need to have a proper vessel to receive the transmission. A statue of the deity needs to be a traditional one, not a 'new age' one and should not be covered in trinkets, crystals etc. You will need a statue, two candles, an altar or work surface, a small cup of honey and a small cup of fresh clean water.

Put the statue on the altar or surface where it will live and light two candles on either side of it. Place your hands upon the statue, one at the head and one at the feet and close your eyes. Go into stillness until your mind is uncluttered and is silent. The key is to not form an image in vision, but to be an open door that allows the power to flow through. You will feel the energy in your hands, or somewhere in your body as the passage begins. It does not take long and once you feel the power pass from you into the statue, pick it up and place your lips to the lips of the statue and breathe into it, finishing the breath with the utterance of the deity's name.

Now the visionary work starts. Standing before the altar/statue, close your eyes and see the altar in vision. See the statue and see the power n it. See the two candles creating a doorway and see the mists beyond/behind the statue. Call out in vision for a priest/ess of the god or goddess to come and work with you, to teach and guide you. Slowly, a shape will appear out of the mists beyond the altar and a priest or priestess will appear. Tell them what you are trying to do and ask for their help.

You will begin to notice that there are other people in a line behind the priest, each one standing behind the other while placing a hand on the priest in front of them. This is the line of succession in the priesthood that the power of the deity will be filtered through: the human inner contacts form a bridge that allows the power of the deity to flow from the depths of the inner temple and connect with the powers of the deity from the outer temple. The two meet in the statue and it 'comes to life'.

Once you see the bright union in the statue, which can appear as brightness, or as a bright pattern, welcome the deity into the statue and offer them the cups of honey and water, doing it in vision and physically at the same time. Place them at the feet of the deity and quietly open your eyes. Light a small candle or tea light before them and offer them incense resin on charcoal (rather than incense sticks which tend to be artificial, low quality etc). Frankincense is a good one to use but it is worth finding out what they like. Modern websites connect all sorts of colours, resins etc to particular deities. These are all modern constructs and have no value in this work. Look to ancient texts, myths, stories and if all else fails, ask them what they like.

The final step is the anointing with oil. I use an oil mix of frankincense, opoponax, and vetiver that I then consecrate for such use. Anoint the forehead, lips, heart and feet of the deity and then leave the room with the candles going. I call this the cooking time: a time when the inner contacts are still working in the room but you are no longer needed. You will feel when it is time to go back in.

That is the 'opening of the door' for contact with the deity. The actual god or goddess power will start to trickle through and the more you work with the contact, the stronger it will become. Do not clutter their space with decorations, magical toys etc: remember it is not a shop display or an artistic presentation; it is a working altar. They will need their candles, an incense burner, two little bowls for gifts/food/drink and any tools that they specifically work with. The tools will be acquired over time or they will ask for them. Anything other than that is going to muddy the filter of the altar and fragment the power. It should be simple, working, and not obviously an altar. Our living room has a series of working altars in the room and no one has ever noticed: it is that simple and basic. No showing off, no drama, no window dressing, just work.

Each day light their lights, ensure they have what they need, and spend just a few minutes in meditation or communion with them. Talk to them, involve them in your daily life and sit with them as you work in vision. This is your foundation deity; they need to be at the heart of your life at home and that can only happen if you build up a relationship with them. The transmission work ensures that it is only the deity or the deity filter/priest that comes through that statue so you do not have to worry about opening doors to random beings.

Build the relationship and once it is established then you can start to work together.

Other Deities

Once you have established a foundation deity, you will find that others come into your orbit over time. Don't go running out to stores to buy lots of different deity statues, let them find their way to you as often the ones that you think intellectually fit together often do not. These days we have become very narrow minded as a culture and like to make things fit together neatly into boxes, but power unfortunately is not that accommodating.

Often the combination of deities that find their way to working with you may seem to be random but on closer inspection they are very connected, not through their attributes, but by geography or cross culture connection from when they were in full power etc. So you may find old Egyptian, Canaanite, Sumerian and Anatolian deities working together, but they will not work with younger generation deities from their own pantheon for example.

Don't fall for the 'all goddesses are one goddess' trap: it is not true. They are akin to humans, all humans are humans, all women are women, but we are all different and work in different ways.

Some of the deities that move in with you will settle in a specific room and you will need to ensure that they will work in harmony with the other deities, ancestors etc that are also in that room. The deeper you go into magic the more your sensitivity to power will increase and if you introduce a power into the wrong space you will most certainly know about it. You will either have nightmares, 'bad feelings', or the house will begin to feel out of balance. If there is imbalance, things will get disruptive in the house with statues falling over, pictures falling off the walls or small fires starting; the deities can really get into pissing contests with each other.

There are two ways that work to deal with this issue. One is to introduce a new deity or magical object by walking around the house, going into each room in turn and standing quietly with the object or statue and seeing how it feels. The nudge can often be like a faint whisper, but most of the time I get a defined, 'no, not in here'.

Another way to check is through using Tarot. I use the Tree of Life spread for this and look at the last card. I ask a question like, 'what would the balance of the house powers, spirits and deities be like if I bring X into this room?' Notice I ask about the effect the newcomer would have, and I don't ask does this power belong here? The reason for that is that you need a clear answer about how something will affect you directly.

It may be the right room for the deity, but if it does not work for you and causes disruption, then it is the wrong choice. You have to be able to work together and the deity has to be able to cooperate with all the other house occupants. You will also find that the dynamics within the house and between all the powers are almost unique to you: the variables are what sex are you, what is the power of the land beneath you, what blood lines flow through you, what ancestors are around you, what animals are in the house and what is the longer term inner path that you are walking (often without realising). So you can see there are no hard and fast rules.

When people say things like, 'this deity must work with that deity and must be housed in this direction because that was how it was in the days of the great temples and that is what their attributes were' etc, they are missing a major magical point. Your house is most unlikely to be upon the same land mass that the original temple of your working deity, it is also not in the same culture, time, setting, nor do you have a whole priesthood keeping all the energetic 'plates spinning'. The dynamic is very different and you need to be mutable to be able to flex and bend with the intricate nuances of power. So reading books on a specific deity etc and their likes/dislikes is going to tell you little of value: a direct relationship with the deity will slowly build the relationship where you will learn a great deal more about the deity power and how it works. Sure you will make mistakes, we all do, but it is part of the process.

One thing to be acutely aware of is if you move house, and it is to a new land or a totally new area, you may find some of the deities change how they behave. The very old primal deities which are usually foundation deities in a pantheon, like Sekhmet, Mut, Enlil, Magna Mater and Shu are manifestations of vast powers and really tend not to change much from land mass to land mass. But other deities, usually the children of the foundation deities, which are essentially powers that have been subdivided in antiquity by the priesthoods, or are localised powers, tend to be more fluid in how their powers work. This means that they may work in one country, but not in another. It's not about them being on their 'own' land, rather it is about being on top of a land power that they can connect with or are compatible with.

So for example, I have moved many times in my life, across continents, oceans etc and have found that as I wander around the world, some of the deities I take with me fall asleep in some countries and become inactive, only to awaken once I move again. Other deities become more powerful, more verbal and express previously unknown attributes and powers when moved onto a new land. Again, it is all unknown magical territory and you have to learn on the hoof. The key is being sensitive to their shifts in power, and that comes from regular work with them.

The basic outer rules are:

1. Let them find what area of the house works for them, they will want to go in a specific direction for a specific reason, so don't for example stick a destroying goddess in the north because that is where all the books say she belongs. She may want to work from another direction for a specific reason or that direction may bring out an aspect of her that you were unaware of.

2. Don't clutter their space with New Age tat. There will be specific things they need so ensure they get them, but don't fall for the altar display routine... it's not a store front or something to show off.

3. Remember you do not have to have altars and all the dressings, for the most part they will blend into your home happily; they wish to live among you and work with you not turn your home into a temple. Most of the working deities in our house would be easily missed; they are in among the books and herbs, not on altars... well, except for one goddess who needs the full deal. Sigh.

4. Most important: this is your living space and your life. They are working powers that you work with, not worship. Sure they deserve respect, honour etc, but make the working boundaries clear...your life is not theirs.

Spirits, Ghosts, Guardians and Ancestors

Once you have built up a working network of deity power in the house, you will come across other potential occupants who are looking for a home. Again this is something that builds over time and cannot be set up like flat pack furniture. The frequency generated in the house by the deities will attract certain types of spirits and will repel those who have no part or purpose in what you are trying to achieve.

Smaller land spirits, faery beings for example, can be attracted like cats . . . leave food out and one will turn up. If you make a point of tending the land around you, talking to the elements, the land, the weather, the plants, then this will get the attention of various beings inhabiting the land around you. Some people build outside shrines, others have a gift patch etc, whatever you do will have some effect and will draw inner beings to your home.

If you have mountains, odd hills, ancient trees etc, anything of natural power around you, then connect with them by visiting them both in person and in vision, introducing yourself and asking the spirits of that place if they need anything. This good mannered approach will catch attention and soon you will have beings turning up needing things, offering things or moving in with you. If one offers to be a guardian for your home in return for shelter/food/song, then all is well. Just ensure that the guardian knows to allow beings, usually ancestors from the area, or from your family, or ghosts to enter the house when they need access to you.

Slowly through trial and error (and there will be errors) you will acquire a family of spirits that live and work with you and this method is the greatest teacher of all: you will find out about inner beings by living among them. In my book *The Exorcist's Handbook*, you will find greater in depth descriptions of various types of beings and how to work with them, what they do, how they act etc.

Balancing the Home Environment

When you live in a home with working deities and spirits, certain considerations have to be taken into account on an almost daily basis. The frequency of the house becomes finely tuned so when something is introduced to the house that is unbalanced or unhealthy, the 'house' will react. This in turn will affect the magician in a variety of ways depending upon their level of sensitivity.

Again it is a matter of experimentation and of being aware of the subtle shifts in the house energy. In the past I have brought in statues which I assumed were simple ornaments but the temple frequency of the house 'activated' them in the strangest of ways which wreaked havoc. I have had the deities of the house react to certain music, foods, people, certain movies etc – it is important to put such reactivity in perspective and not to become neurotic about it. It is all about finding balance and operating within that balance.

I think the bottom line is to use one's common sense and to generally treat a magically working house as a temple, remembering that certain high levels of power are flowing through the space on a day to day basis and to be mindful of what you introduce to the house. Just as you are careful what you expose your children to, so too care has to be taken with the house spirits

It is also worth noting that the guardians that accompany the deities will also be very active: this can be a good thing and a bad thing. On the good side a working house of such magical frequency tends to never get broken into; the guardians do a good job. On the down side, any visitor that you have who is unbalanced, has bad intent, is using drugs in a destructive way or is a person who is parasited or mentally ill will basically get run out of the house pretty quickly. They will feel uncomfortable and you will feel drained.

Another thing to note is that the balance of the powers in the house will shift and change, sometimes in line with the seasons, sometimes it is random and hard to understand why, but the power will ebb and flow, with occasional sudden upsurges of immense power which is usually a signal that you are supposed to be working and everything is lining up ready.

Working this way will not suit those who need a simple rule book with easy steps to follow, nor will it suit those who are nervous, paranoid and self-obsessed. It takes a lot of mutability, a willingness to learn, to flex, to experiment, and the ability to feel shifts of power. However working within this structure will also teach you so much about how deities interact, how powers work together, how guardians operate, and the lessons can be funny, crazy and sometimes terrifying.

When children are added into the mix they learn about power by proxy: you do not have to teach them anything, and they should not be particularly involved with the magical side of living in the house. But being passively exposed to the powers helps them to learn at a deep level about how power works. When my kids were growing up I never mentioned anything to them about magic or the statues around the house, but they were individually drawn to specific ones that they would chat to and sometimes ask for help. The house guardians also watched over them and would warn me if the children were taken sick through the night, or if they needed help. They would also warn me of impending danger around the children.

I have two settings of reaction that I go by, one is sudden adrenal response and the other is fatigue. If there is something dangerous in the house that is a potential threat, magic or otherwise, I will get an immediate adrenal response. If there is something out of balance or unhealthy in the house, I will become suddenly overwhelmed with fatigue. The first response is my body reaction to the guardians reacting, and the second is my inner energy being drained off which triggers a body response. Other people will react differently and it is important to learn your signals and reactions. If there is severe danger, usually you will get a very physical warning, like something literally being thrown at you or a voice shouting for you to wake up.

Here are some examples. Many years ago, my then partner was being stalked by his ex and had many problems with her mental instability. One night I was in the house alone except for my two small children. I was asleep and dreaming happily, when I thought I heard my name called. I was very tired so I just turned over and went back to sleep. A few minutes later I was shouted at in my dream to 'wake up or die' and I saw in my dream fire coming through the letter box (built into the front doors in the UK). I woke up and had an instant adrenal hit. It was 4am and very quiet.

I went downstairs to find my cat sat staring at the front door and growling. I looked out of the curtains and saw my partner's ex with a petrol can coming down the path to the house: she was intending to pour the petrol through the letter box and set fire to the house, with the children in it.

I switched the lights on, pulled the curtains back and stood in full view of her, staring at her. It was enough to frighten her and she ran. If the guardians had not woken me up, we would have likely all burned to death in our sleep.

Another example but less dramatic, was a box of occult/history books I brought home after finding them in a thrift store. Within minutes of getting home I felt sick and disorientated. I could not figure out what was causing it and it did not occur to me that books would have such an effect, so I did a reading to see what was going on as the feeling was very strong. It turned out to be the books. It was not what was in the books, rather where they had been for a long time: they had absorbed something very unbalanced that had become imprinted upon them. The solution was simple; I magically stripped and cleaned the books, and peace was restored within an hour.

A comical example was when a magician was trying to attack me (a total waste of time and energy). A house spirit suddenly made himself known to me, so I went into vision to talk with him. The spirit told me that a magician was attacking me and he had sent a being to carry out the attack. The spirit had the being held at arms length and asked me what I wanted him to do with it. I asked the spirit to hold the being while I observed it so I could see if it was a thought form created by man, or a faery/land being, angelic etc. It was a land being and had been trapped into service. So I freed the being of his servitude and released him out to the moorlands, thinking that would be the end of it.

However the house spirit told me that the fire magic of the attack that had been carried by the being was still in the house, it just had no available 'out' as the being was the aim mechanism. I asked about lighting a fire and feeding it through the fire so it would literally burn itself out. No, not a good idea was the answer. So I asked for suggestions. The house spirit said it could direct the fire magic through the electricity and burn it out that way. So I turned off my computer for the day and unplugged any sensitive electrical equipment, just in time for a light switch to blow and catch fire. I put the fire out immediately and that was the end of that.

Later I tried to figure out why putting the fire magic in the fire was a bad idea, as every encounter with magic is a learning curve. I did some readings to see what would have happened. It showed that instead of it consuming the magic and burning it away safely, as I was expecting, it would have amplified the magic like throwing petrol on a fire. The end result would have been a major house fire. The electrical system was sideways enough from the pure element of fire for it to channel the magic and cause a small fire that was harmless. I learned a lot that day. And it was also a perfect example of the dynamic with certain forms of magical attack: once it is set in motion it cannot always be disengaged and dismantled; it must be safely 'neutralised' or allowed to manifest so it can run its course harmlessly. Some magic can be taken apart and composted, but certain forms of powerful and complex magic has to run a course, the trick is finding a safe and harmless diversion course for it to run.

Downtimes

The other magical dynamic you will discover is the sudden magical silences that occur and often they occur out of the blue. If you try to logically assess how this dynamic works and if it flows for example from lunar cycles or seasonal cycles, you will simply waste a lot of time. Working in this magical way with deities means you need to learn to be fluid with your thinking and approach.

There will be times where the deities suddenly become very active and other times when the silence from them is deafening. I have found that when the powers in the house suddenly become silent, it is not because they have all gone away or shut off, rather it is more that they are suddenly working on a different frequency that we (or I) are unable to operate at. Although sometimes it feels like they are sleeping. They will not want interaction, or candles or offerings or conversation; it will be as if they do not exist. There will be no discernable power flowing around the house and it will feel strangely silent once you have become used to all the background chatter they normally exude. I learned eventually that this is a kind of stealth mode - it is where they are working very hard but in a way that most humans cannot pick up on.

I started to keep a record of this 'stealth mode' and found that it often occurred either when there was a major incident about to happen out in the world, or there was a major incoming attack (one of the down sides of being a visible magician in print, everyone feels they have the right to take a pot shot at someone speaking out). The reasons for the stealth mode would often become apparent a week later. I learned to respect this stealth mode, keep my antenna up and trust their judgement.

What I found very curious was that it would happen before certain major incidents in the world, but not others. I have not gotten to the bottom of why this should be, that a disaster half way around the world elicits a response but one near home or in a different place did not. There is just so much I do not understand about power dynamics and the older I get the more I realise that we actually know so little about how energy and power works.

A lesser occurring dynamic with this crushing silence is when a deity will suddenly go 'to sleep'. They withdraw their powers and you begin to get a sense that you should not be working with them. Again I have learned to just respect the ebb and flow of their power. For example, in spring 2012, my image of the Goddess Tefnut suddenly wanted putting away out of sight. I was dumbfounded because we were still in the midst of a drought (she brings moisture). A week later the rain started to fall and 2012 turned out to be one of the wettest years on record. She was not needed; in fact her presence and any magical interaction with her would have possibly made a bad situation worse.

If such a silence occurs in your own home/magical work, flow with it but keep an eye on it and an eye upon world events. I use Tarot to track if it is a silence that is the result of attack or of world events, and if it is world events I will go in vision and ask if I am needed in service somehow. Usually the answer is no, but occasionally they will give me a job to do.

Magic and Relationships; Bringing a New Partner into the House

This is another aspect of working with a home temple/magical household that we often overlook and can also bring chaos into the home. If a new person is coming to live or even stay in your home, it is a good idea to let the spirits of the house and the deities know there is going to be a new addition to the family, either permanent or simply visiting.

It can be that simple, just tell the house, the spirits, the deities, and keep an eye on the newcomer for a week or so. Failing to do this (as I have more than once) in an active working magical house can have strange consequences ranging from the new comer feeling uncomfortable and sleeping badly, to being attacked in their sleep, constantly getting sick etc. The other annoying thing that can happen if you forget to tell the house guardians that you have a friend staying, is a night of being 'tapped' on the shoulder while you are deeply asleep. You find yourself being awoken by a guardian telling you there is a stranger in the house. Annoying... but they are just doing their job.

It is not a major issue, unless the newcomer is very sensitive, and it is just good manners and common sense. These are the little details that we have lost over the millennia, details that can make a major difference in a magical life.

Summary

Living in a temple house, for me at least, is infinitely preferable to having a separation of working space and home. Through decades of living with the deities and spirits, I have learned to work closely with them without pomp and ceremony, involving them in my daily life and work. This allows a deeper understanding of their powers, needs/ wants, abilities and tides. It is a harder way to work as it keeps you on your toes, and you have to maintain integrity in all that you do. There is no switch off button, no 'time out', but you do learn a lot and get strong!

3
Magic and the Land

Part I: Ground zero. . .
the environment and its powers

The magical inner powers that flow through the land have fascinated humanity since the dawn of time. Power spots became sacred places, people constructed groves, stone circles, temples and some power places were avoided at all costs. This interrelationship between humanity and the power that flows from the land is still a major part of cultures, religions and magical systems to this day.

In this chapter we will look at some different tides of power that flow through the land, to gain a deeper understanding of what it is we are working with. First we will look at how the process of magically connecting and learning evolves; understanding how we operate is a major step towards developing a working practice.

Learning Approaches and Understanding How We Operate

As magicians I think we have all at some point in our lives worked our magic in total isolation, often locked away in a room, ignoring the land and beings around us. This is encouraged by certain streams of magic whereby a temple is constructed indoors, banishing is done, magical circles are set to exclude all except the one spirit to be called, and then we work magic from within that protective bubble. Often the streams of magic worked with have nothing or little in common with the powers that flow from the surrounding land, and the magic is totally disconnected from the tides of power, knowledge and contact that flow from the land all around us.

For magicians who are working with very specific magical methods for very specific results (i.e. results magic) then such isolation works. However, if the magician wishes to expand beyond that paradigm and reach deeper into magic both for practical work and for a better understanding of power, then we have to start to take into account our environment. We need to start asking questions like what power, contact, wisdom and magical pattern is already here in the land? Why is it here? Who is here? What affect are they having on my work? What effect is my work having on the land, the spirits? Can they be a part of my work? And so on.

There are two distinct ways of approaching this. One is to explore the landscape and inner populace of a land area via spirituality/religious format and the other is to explore without the religious/cultural interface but with more of an attitude of what power is here? How does it work and how do I interact with it? Both are extremely valid, both have up sides and down sides and both have their own difficulties. How a magician operates would probably depend upon what stream of magic they were working with and how they personally approach magic.

It also depends upon the development of focus that the magician has acquired over the years. When we first start out in magic, we are like blank pages that take everything in and absorb only a bit. As we progress and begin to specialise with a specific focus of study and work, we begin to narrow our field of understanding so that we become more and more able to see the fine details or undercurrents of an individual section of magic. The down side of that specialisation is it becomes much harder to process patterns that are outside of your own field of perception: you start to see the world around you in a narrower but better focussed way.

That level of specialisation makes for some very interesting realisations once we perceive that what we are seeing/processing in fine detail is not an ultimate 'truth': it is merely a specific pattern. This progression is an emotional, psychological and philosophical process that is an integral part of our magical development.

When we first begin to see the fine detail, the 'machinery' of magic in action, we think we have stumbled upon the truth. The specialisation makes it so much harder to see the same power in action through a different pattern, so we feel 'our' view is 'best' or the real one. This is a higher octave of the messiah trap whereby the magician begins to think they discovered the 'real' path. But when you get a few experienced magicians together who are all from different disciplines and begin to discuss the dynamics behind the magical act, something wonderful happens: you begin to realise that you are all talking about the same thing, just approaching it in a different way with a different language.

Some of these languages are very different and we gravitate to the one that is the most accessible to our mentality. Once the language is well learned and successfully used, it becomes easier to talk to someone who speaks a different language but is working at the same level: the commonalities become obvious. The other side of this coin is the ability to see bullshit even when it is well dressed: the resemblance of power signatures in different paths is very obvious, but so too is the lack of such power.

This repetition of power signatures was a major 'palm to forehead' moment for me that made me step right back and really look at various magical practices, where they came from, why, how and where they were going and why. It also highlighted something to me about human nature, which is the more we look in a very specific way at certain phenomena, the more we rewire our brains to be able to interpret what we are looking at in order to obtain the information we need: we become specialised interpreters. The more we focus in one area, the less accessible other interpretations become.

This revelation made me go back and look at the outer court training of magic and question why certain elements are there. If we have a foundation education in the wider options/expressions of magic, even when we specialise in a particular field, we retain some basis of understanding of the other paths; the neural pathways for that specific learning are established. If we only walk down a narrowed path of learning from day one, we quickly become adept in that path but lose the ability to see the same operational methods in other paths.

This led to an internal discussion with myself (I talk to myself a lot, except around anyone working in mental health!) about why paths develop a certain way, how they develop out of the needs and wants of a populace and how we as modern magicians extract the relevant and discard the irrelevant or dogma. Magic grew out of a religious/spiritual conversation that humanity had with its environment both physical and none physical, and a demand of wants and needs. Keeping that in mind helps us to look at our methods and adjust them to help them evolve.

So, back to working with your own environment and the powers that flow through the land. Working in isolation of our surroundings eventually becomes very limiting and often self-defeating. So what do we do? Often the spiritual connection with our own land has been broken by incoming religions, cultures and modern agendas and it is a struggle to re connect with what is there.

The first instinct is to revert to early religious patterns and try to recreate them. We see this with neo-paganism, neo-druidism, neo-shamanism and the revival of the Saxon religions in Europe. While this is not a bad thing in many ways, it can end up recreating the same dogmatic patterns that are no longer applicable to our land or culture and it can quickly devolve into dressing up and role playing with an added side of psychology.

It also puts us back into the mode of religious patterns rather than evolving into a more mature conversation with the powers around us. But throwing away all the accumulated knowledge and wisdoms in these older religions is also counter productive as many of them originally developed as a result of experience and experiment. So it becomes a matter of looking at the religious/cultural patterns with new eyes; the eyes of magical enquiry rather than worship.

It is also a dynamic that requires something that we humans are not comfortable with, which is taking responsibility. While ever we feel there is a paternal (or maternal) deity to oversee us, protect us and feed us, we are happy to look no further and place our welfare in 'their hands'. In magic, when this reliance on a parent god is enacted, it quickly falls apart as magical power will only work with that dynamic to a point. It also does not take into account that many, (particularly local) deities are not all knowing, all wise, or all powerful. So it all goes wrong and we blame them or ask if we did not sacrifice enough goats (an action which also tends to piss off the neighbours).

If however we approach the local powers and deities in a slightly different way, i.e. be willing to respect and interact with them but take responsibility for ourselves, then an interesting dynamic emerges.

Through taking self-responsibility in a magical relationship with land powers, what tends to happen is that things that you are really capable of handling is left for you to do but what you are not capable of doing and really need is handled for you. So in a way you do end up with a protective deity but the subtle difference takes you out of a parent/child situation and puts you in a chain of action where you become one of a team. Like all teams, you learn to watch each others backs while not babysitting each other.

Researching Your Land

So let's get down to practicalities. Unless you are living on land that has only recently been settled by humans (in which case you are screwed), there will be a variety of resources you can draw upon. One major resource is the local myths, legends and faery tales. These stories are the result of long standing oral traditions and they often have ancient wisdoms, knowledge and experiential learning that has been passed down from generation to generation. These stories, if you know how to look at them, will give you clues to the local powers, deities, ancestors, land qualities etc, and will give clues as how to live and deal with them.

There are many elements that affect magic and the magician, for example the geographic make up of the land. The type of rock, semi precious stones and metals that are in the land beneath and all around you can possibly have an affect upon your magical work, depending upon what you are doing. Many magicians use certain metals and stones in their ritual tools and yet do not think about what is under their feet. So for example certain ritual work will be affected if you are sat (like I am) upon massive outcrops of granite with the added ingredients of lead, copper, tin and silver: a powerful alchemical mix.

The landscape is also important; is it desert? Is it flat forest or mountains or on a fault line? What are the local power herbs and plants? All of these aspects can affect your work depending upon what you are trying to work with and why. Then we get to the inner beings of the land. The first and most obvious are the ancestors who are buried in the land and the ancient ritual sleeper burials; people who actively stay as an inner contact within the land usually for the good of the local tribe.

Then there are the local land spirits/faery beings, deities, elemental beings within the land, the local animal groups, and planetary alignments, key stars etc. There are so many ingredients that make up a magical landscape and taking the time to connect, work with and become acquainted with them can make a major difference in your long term magical projects.

I have lived on different continents and upon different landscapes and as such I have learned how to connect, interact and then leave certain powers. I saw how some similar landscapes had similar power flows and how some land beings did not take well to people living in certain areas. I came across other instances whereby land beings did not want a person to leave and the powers would try to make them stay.

So where do you start? Firstly get as much information as you can about local legends, myths and tales. Read them carefully and look for the main spirit characters, the main land features, who is a 'goodie', who is a 'baddie'. Look at the local faery tales to see what types of beings are described and keep an open mind. Often you have to pull back from the human centric view and the moralising, often inserted at a later date.

These tales will sometimes tell you about the human responsibility within the land collective of beings. They can appear at first to be moral lessons, but at closer inspection they will show some of the ancient dynamics between the land, the beings and humanity, and outline what is expected from the human in return for cooperation. They can also hold clues about how we can work at a very deep level with the land but that such a relationship is finely balanced and dependant upon the human living up to their side of the bargain.

Be careful not to simply discard any myths that seem irrelevant; if you do not find them particularly useful, just file them away as they may become really useful in the future. It is also good to find out what layers of cultural ancestors are on and in the land, and find out for good or bad, what they are about. Not all layers of ancestors are nice or wise, some are very stupid or bloodthirsty so be ready to give them a wide birth if needed.

Geologically, find out what you are sat upon and look up, from an alchemy point of view, how those layers of rock, metals and stone interact with any elements of metal or stone you use in your rituals. It also helps if you find out if there was ever any destructive mining around you and if there was, you may end up having to give a fragment of whatever was mined back or bury some in your garden. The dynamic between metals and stones like gold or quartz in the land, and how the land is affected when they are taken out is an interesting one.

You may find that certain elements that your house is sat upon do not respond well to certain elements within your ritual tools. It really is a matter of 'experiment and see', but stay mindful that many things in your environment will affect how you work.

Working with Beings

The many levels of beings around you that can affect how you work, both for good or bad, can be vast. Doing banishing rituals before you do magic, unless you are doing simple results magic, defeats most of the magical dynamic. Magic does not happen in a vacuum, and if a human is the only being involved in the magical patterning, chances are it will be a piss poor performance.

Magic of any real power is a combination of patterns, energies and beings all interacting at a certain frequency. Together a great deal can be achieved as you are operating as just one link in a long and powerful chain. You learn how to work as a team, how to understand your own limitations and how to trust other beings to do their job. This of course has to be done carefully so that you do not open yourself up to every Tom, Dick and Samael that happens to be passing through.

This is achieved by 'tuning' a working space or even your living space to a certain frequency so that you are operating at a different speed/frequency to lowlife beings; you effectively 'vanish' from their radar. This is discussed in further detail in Chapter 2 so I do not want to repeat myself, but working in combination with different specific beings, powers, inner contacts and ritual actions will ensure that the space/house is always tuned so that you do not become dinner for a hungry local energetic vampire or bottom feeder.

I have also learned through trial and error to develop a good friendship with the 'local spirits' and do whatever I see necessary to help them and the land. I very rarely ask for anything, but when I do, usually in a time of great need, it is immediately there for me. I have also learned from this dynamic that if I am very respectful and helpful, they will often offer help before I have realised that I need it.

Moving on, let's have a look at some of the bigger waves of power that work through the land.

The Tides of Destruction

Over the years I have observed some very interesting phenomena in the various landscapes where I have lived and visited. It took some time for me to realise what it was I was actually observing from a magical point of view and even longer to see the various patterns that seem to emerge in very similar ways upon the land.

My first real encounter with such phenomena, or at least my first awareness of it was in Milwaukee Wisconsin. The area around the great lakes from Chicago up to Milwaukee and across to Madison is littered with ancient burial mounds and when I first discussed this with a Native American who's tribe is from that area, he told me that this area was considered an area of death.

The place where I lived was badly haunted as were areas of the land on the outskirts of Milwaukee. There was a heavy energy to the city that seemed to come and go in waves and at that time I assumed it had something to do with a modern city sat on top of burial grounds. While visiting a burial mound out in the countryside towards Madison, a being appeared and asked if my daughter and I would release something that had been blocked and was building up like a pressure cooker. We agreed and off we went.

My daughter did the contact work and what was released was a wave of female spirits, very warrior like, who spread out across the land. Neither of us were quite sure what to make of it but the moment we finished the work we were told it was time for us to leave that area. Within 2 months fate moved the chess pieces and we did indeed move out of state.

At that time I had no idea what had happened or why, only that it was needful for the land there. I started to do some research into the history of the state and found that the area was renowned for mass murders: Milwaukee had produced more mass murderers that any other single city in its history. I did wonder about how that power mixed with the Sicilian community and its predilection for gang related violence in the form of the mafia in the region's history. Did one feed the other?

Once I moved out of Wisconsin and into Montana I did not give Wisconsin much thought: the place had affected me badly and I was just glad to get out. If I knew then what I know now, I would have stayed longer and worked in more depth to observe, record and discover what natural force was flowing through the land and how the Indians in history would have worked with that force. And as I am writing this, I have just been informed that the river that flowed naturally into the lake at Chicago was reversed by civil engineering in the late 19th century to flow out into the Mississippi basin. Rivers and aquifers play an important part in keeping a land in balance and moderating powers that flow back and forth. Could this have contributed to the unsettled power in that whole area? We will never know but it is a point worth considering. An inspired question would be what is the link between the warrior women/spirits and the water? In the UK and Northern Europe there are powerful links between springs, rivers, wells and female warrior spirits.

Once I settled in the Mission Valley West Montana, I slowly became aware of a strange force that blew through the land on a regular basis. It would come on the tail coats of a storm or a strange wind that would blow through the valley. It felt very different to the power in Milwaukee but it was a tide of destruction that would occasionally blast through the land and leave a string of accidents and deaths in its wake.

It did not occur to me at the time, as I can be incredibly dense sometimes, that the tide of destruction was more feral; it felt more natural simply because that area had only been settled and colonised in the last 100 years, and what civilisation that was there, was very basic and low impact. It was a low population, mainly Indian, with very small towns and settlements.

I began to seriously observe this power. As the tide was about to come, there would be a brief blast of turbulent high wind, often only lasting an hour before it settled. Then a strange energy would descend upon the land that I experienced as a heavy 'lead boots' feeling mingled with a sense of fear. The power would build to become very heavy and adrenal over a period of a few days: people would begin to argue, feel ill and become disorientated. Then something very odd would happen: owls would begin to congregate in quite large numbers and one night I was sat out on my deck listening to trees full of owls calling back and forth.

Sure enough a morning or two later when the energy lifted, there would be news of 'crops' of death in the area. Youngsters killing themselves by driving into trees, into other cars or off roads, drug overdoses, suicides, heart attacks, traffic collisions, shootings, you name it. The longhouse would have a busy precession of wakes and then it would all fall very quiet until the next 'destruction storm' barrelled through.

I talked to various tribal members about the phenomena to see if there were stories, legends or medicine methods that dealt with or at least talked about this occurrence. Elders were quietly consulted and the answer came back as a no, there were no stories or myths about tides of destruction, but the valley was never considered a place for settled living by the tribes; they were herded into the valley by government forces and it became their reservation. The tribes were marched into the Mission valley from their home in the Bitterroot valley. Shortly after that the Jesuits arrived and the tribe was 'converted': tribal activity was squashed immediately and aggressively.

The tribe has only been living in the valley for about 100 years at most as a settled tribe: before that it was a valley that was visited for fruit/ root picking, hunting and major ceremonies. People in the past camped briefly and then moved on: there had not been a settled community there long enough in the past to develop a relationship with this power and learn how to live alongside it.

So over the years that I lived there, I watched this pattern of destruction roll in, scoop up a handful of people and animals, and then barrel out to leave us in peace. At first I used to hunker down and shield myself magically as it passed over but eventually I learned to commune with the power as it passed through, flowing with it and breathing across the land. In vision, I would fly with the wind and see the wind look for 'lights' of life that were fading or somehow looked 'wrong' and the wind would scoop up those souls and carry them off.

It would be easy to psychologise or try to theorise over exactly what was happening, but in truth I learned with such natural expressions to simply take them as I found them and work with them instinctively. That way, my preconceptions, cultural overlay and intellect did not get in the way: I approached these experiences with the mentality of a child who will play, interact and accept without having to analyse, explain and conceptualise something. I found that approach stopped me getting in the way of the experience and allowed my imagination to create an interface whereby I could experience without prejudice what was a perfectly natural phenomenon.

Natural Tide of Death Versus Ritualised

After my experiences in Montana, I became far more observant with the powers that flowed through the land and the tides of death that seemed to roll in and out of particular landscapes. I moved to Nashville where the tides were often linked to the spring storms and tornadoes, but the city and community was too large for me to be able to discern exactly what impact these tides were having on the local population.

In Montana, the local community where I lived was only 600 people, so sudden crops of deaths were easy to observe. However in Nashville, the city was far too large for me to be able to rationally come to any conclusions. I was also immersed in jobs, kids and general life: too many distractions for any real magical observations!

It was not until I returned to live in the UK and moved out to the Dartmoor National Park that I was able to really look closely at this occurrence and work with it magically. Dartmoor is in the south west of England and is a wild moorland area surrounded by sea coasts on the north and south side. The land itself holds the biggest collection of Bronze Age settlements, stone alignments and burial cairns than any other place in England. It is also a land relatively free from Roman ritual overlay of the land and the area where I live has never been touched by the Romans.

Over time I learned which ritual stone alignments seemed to work with death, fertility and sacrifice, and which ones worked with the weather patterns. While exploring these stone circles and alignments near my house, I became acutely aware of how the energy of the land

and the beings that presented themselves responded and interacted both with tides of death and the weather.

To the west of me, going into Cornwall, I came across an inner contact that seemed connected to or residing in a vortex upon the land. This was a place where the trees all leaned into each other in a swirl like pattern, their limbs twisting towards the centre of what appeared and also felt like an energy vortex. I sat in the centre and reached carefully into the land in vision to see what was there. I was very tentative in my approach as although the land here does not have the major power punch that America has, it is still potentially dangerous in these wild areas.

I came across a being that presented itself as a giant who carried a small 'child like' being. My immediate thought was the image of Saint Christopher and I wondered if I had hit a layer of early Christian consciousness in the land. It quickly became obvious that it was far older and was a natural expression of a being in the land that had slowly taken up human form after millennia of interactions with the local community.

The giant was constantly feeding the child and asked me if I had anything to give the child to eat. The giant acted very nervously at the prospect of not having food for this little being and I offered some snacks that I had in my pocket. The child munched happily and the giant breathed a sigh of relief. I was intrigued. I asked the giant what happened when the child did not have food. The giant told me that if the child was not fed, then it began to scream. If the child screamed, storms would gather from the west and kill all who were at sea.

This area has strong fishing communities along the Devon and Cornwall coast and a sudden storm could indeed do serious damage to the local fishing boats and their occupants. I mentioned this to a local magician who lived by the coast and whose family had lived in that area for generations. He recounted tales to me of legends of the screaming winds. Some storms that would come, would whip up winds that would sound like a screaming child as they flowed from the sea onto the cliffs and around the steep narrow valleys. In times past local fishermen's families would say that if the storm screamed, the boats would be sunk and lives would be lost. Hmm... interesting.

I could not find any legends of feeding the child to keep the storms at bay, in the form of offerings to the land or sea, but it is probably through generations of interacting with the local powers that the inner image of a giant/child developed and the screaming sound would signal a particular kind of storm. We could hypothesize until the cows come home, but in the end you deal with what is in front of you and how it interacts with you. I found it fascinating and when I went back to my part of Dartmoor, I began to keep notes on the different types of storms that frequently hit the area. The giant contact did not appear on my part of the moor, and I didn't experience a screaming storm, but I did come across something far more interesting.

Death and Weather:
Talking to the Storm

Once I had settled into my home in Dartmoor, I noticed over the months that the weather patterns for the specific valley I was living in were different to the weather patterns on the rest of the moor. I mentioned it to the locals and they agreed that the little valley had a microclimate all of its own. They had learned to read the signs of the weather over the generations and would use those clues in the running of their farms and livestock. I did not see anything particularly magical about it, more a matter of the layout of the land in relation to the sea, and the shape of the valley itself.

After a couple of years I began to notice that some storms were very different from others. Some storms came in with a feeling of cleaning the land, cleaning the air etc and some felt heavy, oppressive and sometimes dangerous. I also realised that when the heavy oppressive storms came in, I would feel drained, tired and disorientated. One day, the feeling of oppression became too much for me and I decided to do some readings to see what inner dynamic was playing out with these storms.

The result of the readings was a strange one and I was not sure how to interpret them. The readings seemed to show that the storm had a specific consciousness and it was angry. It certainly did feel that way but I wondered if I was reading too much into the situation and if I had missed rational explanations.

Then a really nasty storm came in and hung over the village for days and days. I went to check on some elderly neighbours as the heavy constant rain and wind had trapped them in their houses. All of them, without exception, along with other neighbours I talked to, all complained of feeling drained, agitated and were having nightmares. They also mentioned that when these nasty storms came in and hung around, people would die in the village, usually the pensioners. That really peaked my curiosity as I had assumed the bad feeling was just me, but it seemed that the connections with storms and death were making themselves known again.

So I went back to the cards and asked how I should actively work with this to bring balance. Cards can be used not only for divination but also as a vocabulary and form of communication with spirits. The answer was simple: go and talk to the storm, and let your instincts take over.

Off I went, out into the rain and the wind. I stood on the hill where my house is and stilled myself. I felt an anger and rage in the storm; a hostility to all the people of the village. I reached out in my mind to the storm to get its attention. I was going to talk to the storm in my mind but got a really strong instinct to actually use my voice (the power of utterance). I told the storm how beautiful he was, how wild, how nourishing. The feeling I got back was surprise: storm thought that humans hated it, hated the land and were totally hostile to nature in general.

I spoke out loud, telling the storm how much I loved the land, the trees, the rain, the sun, how I loved tending the creatures, land beings and plants, and how I honoured the wind and all it brought to us. I'm glad no one was standing near as I felt like an idiot; I would have probably been hauled off for being a nutcase.

I got no response from the storm, so I felt I had failed and got the whole thing totally wrong. I went back inside, dripping wet, and got changed. Twenty minutes later, my husband Stuart nodded towards the window and told me that whatever I did, it had worked. I went outside in total awe. The wind had ceased, the rain stopped and the sun came out. And it stayed out. The storm had withdrawn and the heavy aggressive feeling had left the valley.

I was really not sure what to make of this. Although I am a visionary magician, I am also a rational being (no, really!). For any such incident I feel there is usually a logical explanation as well as a magical one; it is just a matter of vocabulary. But I could think of no rational explanation as to why a storm would move on just because I had made friends with it: that only left magical explanations. The next time a nasty storm came in I did the same thing and this time I also sang to the storm. The same thing happened again; the aggressive storm moved swiftly on. I learned to feel the difference between ordinary weather patterns, weather than was coming from imbalance in the climate, and weather that appeared to have consciousness.

The lesson in all of this for me and for you, is that magic is far more than robes and rituals and far more than systems; it is learning how to interact and be in harmony with the forces around us. It is learning how energy and consciousness flows back and forth and to do that you have to approach new learning experiences like a child with an open mind and a willingness to make a fool of yourself. The rationalising can come after the experience. I truly feel that science, particularly physics, will eventually find logical patterns in all of this: the universe is logical and harmonic in its chaos. Magicians use one language and science another. The problem occurs when religion and dogmatic belief on either side come into play.

My experiences with communing with the storms led me on a path of historical research which took me into the realms of ancient history (Enlil et al.) I was beginning to truly understand how humanity first made connections and relationships with storm deities. First would come the communion, then the deity image would develop in the human consciousness as an interface and highway for energy. Keeping it at that level works well. If you take it further and try to control the filter of the deity by manipulating it, then you begin to cause imbalance, but that is another chapter on its own.

The Land and Accidents

Going back to my time in Montana, there was another thing I came across in the land, but I did not understand it fully at the time. For two years I commuted back and forth to a job in Missoula which was around 50 miles from my home. The road I would take, highway 93, is a dangerous road so my antenna had to be in full operation every time I drove. I noticed that there were certain areas on the road where the energy was heavy, dangerous and aggressive. The areas that had this energy were also parts of the road that were particularly dangerous because of the narrowing of the road, the position, cliff faces etc: they were also hot spots for accidents and deaths.

I assumed the horrible feelings at these points were because there had been so many accidents and deaths there over the years. I did toy with the idea that they were bad energy hotspots, but dismissed that thought and went instead for the idea that it was as a result of the deaths there, not the cause of them.

As I moved around the States, I encountered a few of these accident hotspots, or areas where the energy was really nasty, and I would narrowly miss a bad accident or come to one that had just happened. So again, I thought that what I was picking up was a result of accidents not the cause.

It was not until I returned to the UK and was driving a lot that I began to understand something more interesting was happening. I was often driving up and down the M5 between Dartmoor and Bristol and would pass an area that I began to call the black hole. It was an area on the motorway that felt destructive and horrible. The more I drove through that patch the stronger the feeling became. After a year of this, a news flash broke about a massive pile up on the M5 in fog, and it was an accident that had caused many deaths and injuries.

The horrific accident was right in the centre of that black hole that I had picked up on. I had to drive through it again a week later and I was unsettled as to what danger I would be putting myself in.

To my surprise, when I drove through that patch of road, the energy was clear and healthy. Something had built up and dispersed through the accident; the road was now clear. This was not what I had expected. I thought the patch of road was an unhealthy land energy that was a part of the land. Instead, it seemed like it was a vortex or energy patch that had built up and resolved itself with the energy of the crash and subsequent deaths. This was a new experience for me and caused me to look at how land energy, tides of life and death, and the consciousness of the land worked.

Is this what the ancients were working to avoid by tuning the land, interacting with land deities and performing energy exchanges with the power forces? Was that vortex of destruction a purely natural occurrence or was it a result of the road being there and the heavy build up of humanity trucking back and forth? I don't know but it has led me to look far more closely at the forces that flow through us, through the land and through the worlds.

Tides of Weather; the Heralding of Storms

Just as I discovered build ups of death and accident patterns upon the land, I also experienced a very curious thing regarding big storms. I had experienced various weather patterns across the land when I lived in the US and build ups of power upon the land as discussed earlier. I had also experienced being warned and protected by local land beings during dangerous situations, particularly in respect of tornadoes; but that contact was usually immediate, often only an hour before the actual event.

A very curious thing happened that pointed me in the direction of exploring and learning about the long term build up patterns of dangerous and damaging storms. While I was living in Montana, I had been invited to Nashville to work with a magical group of people. It was the end of term in the school I was working at, so that June (2005) off I went to Nashville. While we were in the midst of the magical work something very curious happened.

We were working in a magical pattern of the four directions in vision and ritual, and at one point in the day we were taking turns in walking around the directions and stopping to commune with the contacts in each direction. When it was my turn and I got a particular direction (I cannot remember which one), the being I was attempting to communicate with became distracted and stepped to one side, indicating that I needed to pay attention to something deeper in the direction itself. So I focussed beyond the being and became aware of a vast force of wind; it was destructive, powerful but without emotion. It was so intense it worried me as I felt we were in imminent danger.

I asked the people gathered if hurricanes came through Nashville and I was told that Nashville tended to get the remnants of hurricanes but not really the full on hits; this was more tornado country. I explained what I saw but that I could not ascertain where it was just a natural force in that direction in the land, or whether it was something about to happen; I just could not tell. I could say that a massive force of wind was building up and it was dangerous enough to take many lives.

A few weeks later, hurricane Katrina slammed into the US doing terrible damage and taking many lives. It also had a profound impact upon the nation, the land and the people. I do not know if that pre warning or build up happens for every hurricane or if it was a discernable build up because of the intense inner power of destruction that flowed through that storm. What it did tell me was that such storms gather first as an inner impetus before they express as an outer storm. If we had been people who were properly tuned into the land and powers, and understood the vocabulary of the build up, we could have potentially warned people if we lived in a community that was open to such warnings. Maybe this is something that people in the distant past worked with and were in tune with. It also began to dawn upon me that when someone does a Tarot reading, they are not necessarily 'seeing' the future, rather they are reading the vocabulary of the inner build-up for an outer event that will manifest in the future.

Summary

It does seem that major natural events, weather, death tides and accident hotspots build slowly from an inner perspective and gather inner energy momentum weeks or sometimes months before they express out in the physical world. This is something that I am sure ancestral people long ago were aware of and worked with and we have lost that skill through becoming civilised. It is something however than can be re discovered, learned about and understood for our modern lives today as magicians and a willingness to be open, curious and attentive will develop that long broken bond with the lands around us. We have to relearn all that has been lost and pass on what we learn for the future generations to build upon and develop.

4

Magic and the Land

II: Practical Applications:
The Gardens and the Groves

In the last chapter we looked at some of the power manifestations that flow naturally upon and within the land. In this chapter we will look at practical ways a magician can work directly with the land powers and how a magical relationship between the land and the magician can be forged.

There are a variety of ways that a magician can work with land powers and what methods you use depends upon what your magical practice is, what you are trying to achieve and what level of power you are willing to immerse yourself in. Working with the land can go from being very simple interactions with the environment, to the other extreme which is a sacrificial upholding of the land through the body until death (and then possibly becoming a sleeper).

In between those two extremes are layers of magic that can be worked with and put into action; it all depends upon what you are trying to achieve and why. This type of work tends to move way from ritual magic and becomes more shamanic or faery orientated just by nature of the powers you are working with and the environment around you.

Let's look at different magical dynamics for working with the land both in a personal magical use all the way through to long term generational magical service.

Nurturing the Land

Our cultural attitude towards the land has been heavily influenced by the passage in the Pentateuch, Genesis 1:26 -

Then God said, "Let us make man[a] in our image, after our likeness. And let them have dominion over the fish of the sea and over the birds of the heavens and over the livestock and over all the earth and over every creeping thing that creeps on the earth."

That one word, dominion, has had terrible far reaching consequences in our relationship with nature and the land around us. We have raped and pillaged our environment and all the creatures that exist around us in a selfish orgy of resources. But if we change that one word 'dominion' for 'stewardship', then a very different story can be told.

We are unique as a species in that we can reach beyond our everyday consciousness and manipulate power, energy, and inner contact to build, destroy or simply commune with the invisible Divine forces around us: the act of magic. It is time to evolve beyond a mindless stripping and controlling of everything around us and instead move towards a more mutually respectful and beneficial relationship with the world around us.

There is a movement within spirituality and magic that calls for a non interference with nature, which is a noble thought but is not realistic and certainly not balanced. We have enclosed land, killed predators, fostered beneficial plants and edible animals over non edible ones. We have built highways, cities etc: this is the reality that we live in and we have to work within that reality. This can be done in practical ways and in magical ways.

The revival of nature worship and neo-shamanism by people who essentially are civilised, well resourced and generally out of touch with the harsh reality of nature has coloured magical practice today in a variety of subtle and not so subtle ways. A simple example is one regarding land management. A couple of years ago I met someone who had just finished an environmental degree, moved from London into the country and bought a few acres of forest. He wanted to live as naturally as possible on the land with his family and planned upon building a house in the woods and letting the land govern itself. He felt that the faery beings within the land would keep the land in balance: a quaint idea and totally devoid of understanding of how nature worked.

I went to visit him and his family after a year and he bemoaned the fact that although the land was covered in trees, no herbs grew, no plants etc and the house they had built was damp, dark and difficult to live in. I pointed out to him that although his heart was in the right place, he needed to step back and look at how the land would have been if the house, fences, dogs and near by town were not there. He did not understand what I was talking about.

If that patch of land was completely natural, it would have had deer to keep the saplings in check and strip bark from some trees to slow their growth down and let sunlight get to the ground. The boar would have grazed the forest floor which also kept brush down and allowed plants to grow, wolves would have kept the deer in check, fires would have burned up the brush and stimulated new growth, the local river would have flooded across that patch of land (it had been diverted and the area was an old flood plain) to replenish the soil and again keep certain growth in check. The list was endless. Instead, the fenced acreage and lack of land management resulted in overgrowth of the forest and brush build up on the forest floor which in turn suppressed plants, turning the land bitter: it was slowly killing itself.

The trees were densely packed and were all dying. His house got no light and the family were generally miserable.

We have to work with what we have in reality and we have to compensate for the changes our presence makes. It can make for very interesting living and can either be very simple or as magically complicated as we wish to make it if we use our common sense. The first trick is to stand outside of mainstream thinking and also the comfortable 'cuteness' that an abundance of resources has allowed us. We can be all compassionate and loving to trees, birds and animals when we have full bellies and a roof over our heads. But that is not true nature. When resources are very low, then the fight for survival resumes. Keep that in mind when you plan your magical action: are you looking at the land with a true perspective or through the lens of the 'Disney channel'?

Magical Gardening

The simplest way of working with the land is often the most profound teacher, though it is not very glamorous. This is the most basic way to work with the land but it is also the most powerful. Once you have done deep inner work with the weather tides, the land beings etc, returning to this method brings a new level of depth and awareness of land power through a very simple almost non magical action.

It can be a very small part of magical practice or it can be the only magical action a person wishes to take upon the land. Either way it will teach you a great deal about how the land, the plants and the animals all jostle in a fight for survival. That battle for survival is like base camp for magical gardening, but it can step beyond that into much deeper magical and power dynamics.

The first step of magical work with the land is to tend a garden. Most of us these days think of gardens as lawn, herb and flower patches with few if any weeds, raised beds, garden ornaments, etc. A lot of gardens like that quickly become sterile: they are inner wastelands. A lawn is a sterile environment and serves no purpose other than sitting on. A heavily weeded garden is out of balance and is akin to having a room full of very uptight people that have nothing in common with each other. Also bear in mind a lot of flower species are ones that have been heavily genetically modified and have little if any nature function left in them: they are very beautiful but it is like looking at a beautiful caged bird.

On a practical level, the steps to take would be to first find out what plants would have grown naturally in your area. Find out which native species attracts bees, birds, insects, butterflies etc. Look into what are the poisons, what are the medicinal, what are the functional weeds that strengthen the soil and the other plants around them. We have a very odd mentality as humans in that when we grow herbs or food, we tend to grow them in a line, all the same plant in one big patch and weed around them furiously. It really is the worst thing you can do.

My mother was an amazing gardener and could grow just about anything. One of her rules was, scatter things around, find out which plants make friends and support the delicate ones, watch to see which ones are the bullies, and finally sing to your garden. It worked and I began to apply her reasoning to the work I was doing, and I had wonderful results. I also learned a great deal about the consciousness of plants by observing, listening, and watching inner interactions between them – it truly is fascinating and rather shocking. I knew plants had some form of consciousness, I just had not realised quite how much and how sophisticated it was.

My garden looks like a patch of chaos, but it is healthy, pest resistant and fertile. I got rid of ornamental bushes, grass and invasive species, planted native plants, medicinal/magical herbs and poisons, and let the dandelions, chickweed etc grow in between them. My mother taught me that weeds, when kept in balance, help to protect delicate plants by providing strength and 'buddy' immunity from pests. It worked! So my garden looks rather overgrown and unkempt (and pisses off the neighbours) but in reality it is healthy and as balanced as I can get it.

The next step, which is the first magical step, is the power of intent. When you train up in visionary or ritual magic, the power of focus of intent becomes honed to a fine point. You can cast your power of thought into a focussed direct line and allow power to flow down that line. When I go out into the garden, I go out with the magical intent of tending the surrounding landscape and all who live there.

A plant which is young, delicate or not quite established, but has great magical/medicinal potential must be fostered and cared for. A plant that grows out of control and is swamping all the others must be cut back. But when that action is done magically, it is done with the intent that the power of the action is magically mirrored across the land. Harvesting of herbs is done carefully, and at the right time, to ensure the healthy survival of the plant while you take some of it but not all. It is like working with a homeopathic magical intent: what you do in the garden from an inner point of view spreads a corresponding potential for action across the land. It is the simplest and most basic of inner dynamics.

Tapping into Hot Spots

This is where real earth magic begins and where the magician can really begin to develop skills, while at the same time learning how to tune an area of land in order to work with it magically. This would be the introductory foundational action for building a temple or a sacred grove, or working to affect balance upon the land, species, weather, or to illicit protection in times of great danger etc. Temples, stone alignments and groves do not become magical or powerful by nature of their building, but by finding a power spot upon the land, the tuning of that land, the contacting of the powers there and the opening of the gates of that power spot.

Most temples and stone circles in the ancient past were positioned with great care as they were mediators of the power that flowed through a specific land mass/power spot. A degenerate or reverse form of this wisdom can be observed in the early Christian church: they positioned churches upon sacred pagan places, power spots, burials and former temples in an attempt to suppress what was underneath.

The following methods can be used for both 'virgin' powers spots, i.e. places that have had no previous ritual working or construction upon them, and for land that has no particularly known power point, but is to be fostered and used for magical purpose.

The first step is identifying a hotspot or power spot upon the land. There are more about that we often realise and some turn up in the strangest of places. If you are psychically sensitive, then you will find yourself drawn to power spots and will either be drawn in or repelled by the power – either reaction is good and can be worked with. Dowsing is also a good way to identify power spots and for those who are not psychic and not dowsers, looking into local legends, myths and stories regarding the land area will often give you clues.

Usually though, if you are a magician working with the inner contacts and the land, you will be dragged kicking and screaming at some point to a hotspot and told to work with it; the key is to listen carefully to very faint voices that try to nudge you to visit a particular area.

The second step is to ascertain what sort of power is running through that hotspot. Again this can be easy or really hard depending upon the magician's level of inner sight, instinct, connectedness and stillness. The best and easiest way is to go and lie upon the land. Still yourself internally until you are deep in the void, in stillness, and slowly bring your consciousness back to your body and the land. As you do that, be acutely aware of tiny changes in how your mind and body react to the land and then how your emotions change.

How you react should tell you a great deal about what type of site it is. If you feel a rush of excitement, or expansion of energy, or a sense of being taller than you are, then chances are the land power at that spot is about energy *output* i.e. regeneration/healing, fertility/growth, or a pressure point for the weather. If you feel sleepy, drained, on alert and in danger, then it is most likely an energy *input* site i.e. it is pulling energy from the beings, people and creatures around it. In such case it is more likely to be a power spot for death, storms, disease or an entrance to the Underworld. If it is an input site, don't necessarily shy away from it: you can learn a great deal of very important magical knowledge from Underworld, death, disease or storm power points. They are a part and parcel of existence: creation and destruction are powers that should be worked with equally across the lifetime of a magician.

The third step is figuring out what type of pattern would be appropriate to develop over the power spot and that depends on the power, the land around you and your agenda or intent. One important rule to remember if you are going to develop a magical pattern to tune a hot spot (which could last for a long time) – if you build it, you are responsible. If you create chaos, you are responsible: you will potentially 'carry the energetic can'. With that in mind, if you are not intending to work with the site for a long period of time, i.e. years/ decades, but rather just for a few months or weeks, then the pattern you establish magically must reflect that. You use simple construction for short term use, clean it up afterwards and disperse the power when you have finished. If you are planning long term work, then the construction need to be built to last and to potentially hold vast amounts of power (you never know!).

Let's look at simple short term construction first. This would be a construction lightly built for making contact with local powers, dealing with a specific job and then closing down.

Short Term Construction

The first action is the creation of the anchor point, the area which acts as a gate to the sacred space and grounds the guardian position - it literally anchors the magical construction to the land. To establish this, first work in vision while sitting upon the land. It is a very simple action: sit and go into stillness/silence and when you are still, be aware of the land around you and particularly the patch of land you are on. See yourself in vision standing up and walking around the four compass points of the land you are working on and be aware of the subtle feel of the energies in each direction. Hold the intention of trying to find the 'gateway': the area where power flows freely from the inner worlds to the outer world.

It can be a subtle sense, almost like a whisper, or it can be a strong force that makes itself known. Having established the 'power in' gateway, you then need to find the 'power out' gate; which direction does the power flow out of? Notice I have not included 'down' or 'up'. This is deliberate: when building a sacred or magical working space, you use down or up as fuel points for the pattern you are constructing: if the pattern is for the future, you draw down power from above. If the pattern is about ancestors and invigorating them, or about death, or the past, then 'down' is where you draw power from.

Once you have established 'in' and 'out' gates then you need to start building up the pattern itself. This is very easy but can be time consuming. The key to this is mental focus of intent along with stillness: do not let your mind wander but keep a clear mind as you work. Starting in whatever direction of east, south, west or north that the 'in power' gate is in, stand before the gate and 'see' a gate or two standing stones that create a doorway. Imagine in your mind the power flowing in through the gate. Then move on to the next direction, working clockwise, and imagine a stone or pillar or stone altar there marking the threshold. Ensure that you build up the 'power out' gate wherever it makes itself known to you. Continue this method until you are back at the 'in' gate and go around again, repeating the process.

This action builds an inner template using the imagination, and because you work magically with intent, the imagined template begins to form an energetic impression upon the land. This in turn informs the spirits and powers within the land what your intentions are and what you are trying to achieve. The pattern you establish upon the land becomes a vehicle for action and the power becomes the fuel: you are the driver.

Depending upon the response from the land, you may have to repeat this simple exercise a few times over the span of days or weeks to build it up or it may power up and pull into focus straight away. Personally I have found that if what you are planning to do is needful for the land/people/creatures/weather etc, the power comes into focus almost immediately and the whole thing is finished over a day or two.

When the pattern is established and you can feel it upon the land as you walk around the circle starting in the east and progressing clockwise until you reach the north, then it is time to get to work. Position yourself in the centre with your back to the 'in' gate. Stand (not sit) and go in vision into stillness, into the void, to quieten your mind and body down. When you are still, focus upon your task and see in your imagination the gate behind you, the gate before you, the direction to your right, the direction to your left, be aware of the ancestors beneath your feet and the powers of the stars above you. Draw your attention to your own centre, and see your centre as a light, an almost formless light that will allow things to pass through it.

With that focus, using your inner vision, see the power flow into the working area through the 'in gate'; channel it through you, through your centre. See energy flowing into you from below or above and see the directions on either side of you as strong boundaries upholding you. When all the threads of power have been brought together, focus them like a beam and see that beam flowing through the 'out gate'.

As the power flows out of the out gate, 'see' where the power is to be sent beyond the gate and utter your intent for the power, i.e., "I send you out into the world to bring about whatever change is necessary for balance of/protection of etc." Notice that the utterance does not specify what that change should be, only that you are asking for what is necessary. For example if the action is about protecting someone or a place, then it is whatever is needful to achieve that.

This open ended way of working allows the power to find the weak spot in the situation and fill it to bring about change. After that it will work to its own time and way, but it will be achieved. That way of working is very simple but also very difficult: it uses no beings, no inner contacts, no tools, no weaving of rituals beyond establishing gates. You become the pontiff of power, the bridge that gathers energy and focuses it in a defined way for a specific purpose. If you have done little or no visionary magic, then chances are your mind is not yet focussed enough and you are not connected enough from an inner contact point of view to be able to gather that power and send it. But if you have established a solid working practice in visionary magic then this way of working can be very powerful. But it uses no additional workers or spirits; it is just you, the land and power.

Once the work has been done, then the pattern needs breaking up and dispersing. This enables the land to go back to its natural flow and also ensures that no one else can stumble across your work and tap into it. The best way I have found to do this is to not go back around and dismantle the gates and thresholds, but to use a dispersal pattern that is a natural action in the weather and the land. This ensures the patterns and powers are broken up naturally and flow back into their natural channels.

It is a very simple method but very effective. Stand in the centre of the pattern and begin to turn. It does not matter which way you turn and your body will have a natural inclination to go one way or the other. As you turn, outstretch your arms while imagining that your arms extend far beyond you and are knocking over the gates and gathering the power up, a bit like a tornado or whirlwind. Begin to turn faster; see the power and the pattern broken up and being sucked up to a column that you are the centre of. Once everything is in the column, stop and immediately begin to turn in the opposite direction. Let the power flow out through your hands, spreading it out across the land at random. It may also flow up to the sky or down into the earth through you. When you feel it has all gone, stop. It's that simple.

This method draws upon flows of power and energy that are natural and are a part of the land. It leaves no echo, does no damage and achieves its goal while working with the land.

Note: If you are naturally psychic and wish to work as naturally as possible, then once a power spot has been identified, simply make friends with spirits and powers in the land. Walk around the land and make friends with those spirits and ancestors who are drawn to you; tell them what you are trying to achieve and ask for their help. Follow the lead that they give and simply hold the intent of action while standing upon the land. Just be very clear in your intent and what help you need. The rest happens organically and uses no magical patterns. It is a simple and powerful way to work in union with all the beings upon the land but only really works if you can easily connect with different beings and if your intent fits what they are willing to work with.

Longer Term Construction: Building a Sacred Grove

This technique can be used when you are trying to develop a sacred working/temple space from scratch upon the land. It is only used when the type of space you are trying to build is one that will be dedicated to working with the powers of nature, so it would not be a suitable method to use if you were trying to establish a new ritual temple or deity working space that uses ritual/temple style magic. This is more of a method used for building spaces that would operate similarly to stone circles, medicine wheels, sacred groves etc: spaces that work with the land powers, the weather and the ancestors.

The methods for identifying the space and building the entrance 'gate' are the same as the methods used that are described in the 'tapping into Hotspots' section above. After that the technique diverges along a slightly different path. Building a sacred working space upon the land is the foundation of a focussed working space that should withstand the ravages of time. It will not be as long lasting as the Neolithic and Bronze Age sacred sites scattered across the world, but it should at least last for your lifetime and will continue as long as it is worked with.

The building of a sacred space is essentially identifying a power spot, tuning it to a working pattern, bringing in land spirits, ancestors and elemental powers and weaving them all together in a balanced and harmonic pattern. How you construct the site both inner and outer, the beings you work with and the actual work you do in the space will decide how successful the site will be over time. It is all a matter of keeping balance, working respectfully with the spirits and cooperating rather than commanding.

Once the gate is 'built' and the four cardinal directions are also established, then it is time to call in the spirits and beings to assist with both the construction and the work itself. Working in a clockwise fashion, go to the first direction past the gate (so if the gate is in the north, then start in the east etc). Stand in the direction and first work in vision. Using inner vision, see a directional threshold in the form of a stone and see beyond the threshold out into the inner landscape of the land. Using the power of utterance, use of the breath with magical intent, call out for a spirit of the land to join you, one who is willing to work with you to build this sacred place. See in your imagination a being appear in the distance and come walking towards you.

When the being reaches you, tell them who you are, who your family is, what land you were born on, where you live now and what you are trying to achieve. Tell them what work you want to create upon the land and why. If the being agrees with what you are trying to do, they will agree to stay and work with you. They may indicate to you what type of being they are, what skills they have and what they may want in return.

If no being appears in your mind, do not force it. Not every direction on every patch of land has a being that will be forthcoming. Remember, your imagination is only an interface, it sends out signals that spirits can decipher and creates a window in your consciousness whereby the beings can interface with you. If you try and force an image or happening, the contact will shut down. It is a delicate balancing act to create a mental interface without allowing the imagination full control.

Once contact is established, move clockwise onto the next threshold. Repeat the same exercise in each direction until you come back to the gate. The only difference with the gate is you put out a call for two beings to act as guardians and threshold keepers. Again do not try to form what they are, or what they look like, just allow them to commune with you through your own mind and show you what they look like, or show you an image from your own mind that tells you what their powers and abilities are.

Now that the inner contacts are established it is time to ritually build the space. This action plants a physical pattern upon the space and anchors it to the land so that power can flow from inner to outer and outer to inner. Each direction will need a stone to act as a threshold marker/link, and the gate will need two stones to act as the gate posts. Getting the right stone is very important as some stones can bring a strong presence or resonance into the space. To find the right stone, start by standing in the east. Ask the contact to guide you to the stone needed for the east. Cross over the threshold and physically walk into that direction while trying to keep an awareness of the land around you.

Let your instincts and the contact guide you as you walk around the land until you find the right stone. You will be drawn to an area and eventually the right stone. If you handle it or touch it, it will feel very different energetically to all the other stones around you. If the stone needed is far away, which sometimes happens, you will get a strange compulsion to set off in your car or on foot to a specific spot.

When you have found the stone, (it does not matter how big or small it is, rather it is important that it is the right one) tell the stone what you are going to do. This is very important: often smaller land beings (faeries) inhabit stones and you do not want to anger them by being disrespectful. It is worth taking time with this part of the work: commune with the stone to ascertain if beings are inhabiting it and if they are, talk to them; ask them if they want to join you and if not, ask if they need anything from you.

When all negotiations are suitably finished, take the stone to the site and put it in the direction. Make sure you always enter the space always from the 'in' gate, even if there is no marker stones there yet: it is important to establish the flow within the space with the regularity of your actions. Walk a full circle and come to rest in front of the direction the stone belongs in. Place the stone on the ground and stand or kneel before it, placing your hands upon the stone. In your inner vision call out to or see the spirit/contact of that direction come towards you, pass through you and into the stone. They are not trapped there and will not be always there; what you are doing is establishing a physical anchor in the site for that being. You can use the stone in future to make energetic physical contact with the being, and the being will leave a thread of themselves in the stone so that they flow back and forth to the site.

Saying that, it has happened to me whereby the spirit goes right into the stone and stays there, living in the stone. If that happens, then that is how that being prefers to work and they will establish their energies within the structure of the site. You do come across this sort of thing occasionally in stone alignments where the stones are still housing spirits that sleep within the stones.

You need to repeat this action in each direction and also for the two gate stones at the entrance. It can take some time and also some muscle work if the stones that the spirits want are big ones. It might bode well to have others working with you to lessen the load and to also assist in the construction. If there is a group of experienced magical workers then each of you can do a direction which makes life a lot easier and less sweaty!

Once the stones are in place and the contacts/spirits are all connected to the stones, then the threshold of the gate needs to be sealed. This is simply but powerfully done. Stand at the gate on the threshold and be aware of the beings on either side of you. This part is all physical and not visionary as it seals the place in the physical realm. Call out to the wind,

"I have built this sacred temple of the land with the rocks of the earth, the spirits of the land and by the will of my heart. I ask that you, wind that blows

through the land, wind that brings weather, wind that brings life, to bear witness to this sealing. I ask the sun and stars above, the sun that brings warmth and strength to us, and the stars that seed the future of all things to witness this sealing, I ask the Great Mother beneath my feet, She who gives of her stones, She who birthed me, She who holds all the ancestors in her rich earth, I ask the Great Mother to witness this sealing. This is the threshold of the sacred grove, and I charge the guardians to uphold this space; none who have destructive or unbalanced intent may enter, but those who love the land and wish to serve shall be upheld within this space."

When you have spoken, prick or cut your finger and drip your blood in a line between the two guardians. This informs the guardians of the ground rules you are establishing and your blood connects you to the site. If anything powerful is happening in the grove, you will get an energetic 'pull' to visit the site.

Starting Work

To operate the grove, you will need a central element to work with, to draw the power in and to act as an access route for the land spirits around the grove. This can be a flame in a fire bowl (to protect the land from the fire) or a bowl of water. Sometimes in the past a person was used; they would be ritually slain and buried in the centre of the grove or at the threshold to act as an intermediary. These days, killing your granny and burying her in the grove is not socially acceptable, so fire or water is a better modern approach!

To begin work, you would start in the centre with the element. Still yourself before the element, until your mind is completely silent (going into the void). Using inner vision, see yourself get up and go (clockwise) to the first direction after the gate and stand before the stone. Call out for the contact of that direction to come to the stone and establish the visionary contact; greet them and ask them to work with you. Repeat the action in the other directions until you get to the gateway. Acknowledge the guardians and ask that they allow the deity power (could be a local land goddess, a storm god etc) to flow freely in and out of the gate.

Then it is time, once the contacts are all primed, to begin work. Start at the first direction again and this time working ritually; stand before the first stone and call out (using your voice) your intent to work, and what you ask of the powers. Keep the request simple and be aware that the more you try and condition the action and outcome, the more restricted the magic will be.

So for example if you are trying to work with a recent disaster upon the land, you would state that you wished to work to achieve whatever is needful to bring balance to that situation and the beings/ powers involved. So for example if there has been a mass shooting, or murder or a terrible accident, you would work with the directional contacts to bring balance. That may entail gathering up the souls of the dead and providing a path whereby the souls can flow into the grove, through you and into the fire. This would guide them into the void so that they can begin their death journey: often people killed in such circumstances become 'stuck' on the land. This can often be directly experienced by visiting a disaster area and feeling the energetic impact and the trapped unhealthy energy.

If you were doing such a task, you and the contacts of the grove would create a circle, the guardians would hold the gates open for the dead, and you would stand between the gates and the fire, allowing the souls to bridge through you into the fire.

On the other hand if you were aware of the disaster area being imbalanced and lots of unhealthy beings/spirits drawn to that area, you would work with the contacts and a local deity to restore the order of the land, which would happen either by beings of an opposing power being drawn from the directions on to the affected land, or the re establishing of the deity power upon the land.

The possible techniques to use are endless and you need to develop a working method that spans vision, ritual and utterance that works for you. The key is intent, focus and building up the energy pattern in the grove by constantly walking around the directions and communing with each of the contacts in vision. It establishes a simple working pattern that takes on its own frequency which in turn shuts out parasitical and unhealthy beings.

If you work with this method on the land you will find that the grove slowly takes on a life of its own and the more you work around the directions, the more you 'tune' it, the stronger the contacts become. Over a period of years you will find that the grove starts to work with you through dreams, through every day life, and that it powers up the moment you stand within it.

Just don't make the mistake of trying to 'dress' the grove in New Age trinkets, crystals, incense etc. You are working with pure nature, so keep it that way. Often the beings within the stones like simple food offerings (bread, nuts, fruit, things that would not harm the local creatures or birds), or olive oil or wine poured over them (the Romans were really into that action).

We are at the stage of magical development in our time where we are trying to re learn what was lost; a fluid organic way of working as opposed to grimoire, heavily crafted ritual etc. Such an over organised way of working often works in conflict to the land and spirits rather than in union with them. Let the grove and its spirits teach you how to work successfully.

After a working session, go back around the directions and thank the contacts and ask if they need anything doing. This is very important that you establish a two way system of work: the grove work is not all about you and your agenda: it is a working interface between you and the land. The land spirits will at times ask you to do things for them and you may find that over time, the grove develops as an interface of constant magical flow between you and the land. It becomes your work station in service to the land.

Always, at the end of a session, leave a gift for the grove spirits. This can take the form of honey, tobacco, bread, mead etc, things that degrade, that have a strong energy and will not kill or damage local creatures. Leave it in the centre or distribute it out between the directions. Always acknowledge the guardians every time you walk in and out of the grove, and place your hand upon their stones and let them take some energy from you.

It is also good practice to build up a friendship relationship with the grove and spirits there. This is done by simply going to the grove to hang out there, be in the space while you read or sleep, or just sit and be still. Take bread/honey gifts, and if a land deity has established themselves in the grove, go to honour them and just be with them. Do not be overly formal with a grove: although it is a magical space it is also a natural space; the relationship between the magician and the space is informal, often intense and will develop organically into a closely bonded relationship. Listen to the grove, listen to the spirits and the deity, they will talk to you through your thoughts, instincts, dreams and through animals/birds. And do not try to 'own' the grove. It is a sacred land space and at some point it will call to others to come and work. If you find inappropriate gifts of things left in the grove, just quietly take them out and dispose of them unless they are gifts that are appropriate. (i.e. take out plastic ribbons, candles, etc but leave food, bones, etc).

To finish, I will give you an example of a sacred grove that called to me. I think I have talked about this a little bit in a previous book, but it is pertinent to this chapter (and saves you having to sift through my books to find it).

The Story of Medicine Wheel

When I lived in Montana, I used to run errands for tribal elders and one weekend I was asked to take some supplies in my truck to a powwow on the Crow Agency Indian Reservation which sits on the border between Montana and Wyoming. When I looked on a map for the best route, I noticed a mountain called Medicine Mountain that was near by. I made plans to go back home via Yellowstone Park so I could visit this mountain, which seemed to be pulling at me for some reason. I mentioned it to one of the tribal elders and he told me about medicine wheel, a sacred site up on the mountain. He asked if I intended to go there and I said yes, unless he felt there was a reason I should not.

He said it would be fine and I could do him a favour. Would I be willing to take a prayer bag there from his family and pray for them? I felt honoured just to be asked, and of course I agreed. By the time the hour arrived for the trip, I had 3 medicine bags to take there as gifts for the sacred site, some sage and 'husks' (a local sacred root) as a gift to the site, and a beautifully crafted medicine wheel given to me by one of the elders to hang in the truck, to protect me. So what started as a casual idea rapidly turned into something of a pilgrimage.

I dropped off the supplies at the Crow Agency and set off up Medicine Mountain. As my truck struggled with the steep mountain roads, I watched with foreboding as the bright warm summer sunshine slowly turned to dark clouds and cold. As it was summer I was dressed in T-shirt and jeans, but the higher my truck inched up the steep mountain road, the colder it became until I was seeing snow at the sides of the road. Uh oh.

I finally arrived at the place where I could park the truck, as the rest of the journey had to be done on foot. I groaned outwardly when I saw other trucks there; I had hoped to do this alone, undisturbed. A faint voice in my head told me to wait. To park up, roll a cigarette and just wait. So I did. Within minutes the dark clouds really gathered and snow began falling (in summer!). I was at 9,000 feet and it had not occurred to me that the weather might have been colder (duh). I had just finished my cigarette when I saw people running down the mountain path to the trucks, trying to get out of the blizzard that was slowly building. Within fifteen minutes I was alone (and cold).

Luckily, I had some Indian blankets in the truck with me, a habit I had gotten into after being caught by cold weather in the Montana wilderness before. I gathered the gifts into a backpack, threw two blankets over myself and began the hike up the mountain to the wheel.

I could barely see where I was going for the snow but every step I took, voices challenged me and were all around me asking me who I was, why I was going there, what were my intentions. The voices got stronger and stronger, so I answered: I told them out loud who my family was and that I was not Indian (nor wanted to be), I told them about the medicine bags I was carrying with prayers from the Salish elders, about my own gifts and prayers, and that I intended to honour the site.

When I finally arrived at the top of the trail, the medicine wheel was laid out on a ledge and at nearly 10,000 ft it felt like the edge of the world. I asked the wheel guardians permission to enter and realised that they could very well say no, in which case I would have to say the prayers where I stood, leave the bags by the perimeter and go. Thankfully they said yes. I cautiously climbed into the centre of the wheel, being very careful not to dislodge the ritual pattern laid out in stones, and sat down. I laid the medicine bags from the elders in front of me and began prayers for them and for an ancestor of mine who was buried on the reservation. I had wrapped one blanket around myself and one draped over my head like a veil, so that I would be warm but still able to see. After the prayers, I closed my eyes and went into vision.

I had a long and detailed visionary interaction with an elderly woman, some of which I did not at that time understand, but it was vivid enough that I would remember. It did not seem to take that much time and thankfully the snow was easing up a bit. When I finished I left a gift of tobacco and husks and hung the medicine bags on the posts near by. I got a strong urge to sing, which is most unusual for me as I sing like a strangled cat, but the urge was strong, as if it was something the spirits wanted. So I sang the spirits a song from my childhood: a Sean Nos song. The Sean Nos songs are old Irish ballads, myths and poems sung without instrument in a highly stylised way that reaches far back in time. I was not sure what reaction a foreign song would get, but they did seem to like it. I got a feeling of benevolence, almost like an adult smiling at a child who is saying all the wrong things but has the right intent.

I set off in the snow and worked my way back down to the truck. I did not feel too cold and I realised I had not felt the cold at all while I had been sat in the snow. The shock came when I got back in the truck. On firing up the engine, I saw that I had been sat on the mountain in the snow for three hours! I thought I had only been sat for about ten minutes, with half an hour to get up there and same coming back down.

My experience with the old woman in the wheel triggered things that changed my life and my magic most profoundly. The wheel itself was very powerful and very ancient: it had been built to last over millennia and its pulse still beat loudly enough for anyone listening to hear it. This is a perfect example of a constructed grove/site that does not exclude those who need to touch base with its power, or to pass by and offer work, or to go to honour the land – it was well guarded, well tuned and was willing to work with me despite my being from a foreign land. And that is another important point to remember with these ancient powers and places: they do not see race, colour, creed or culture.

But they do see respect and integrity. When that particular wheel was built, there were no issues with invaders, colonisers or New Age co-opting of traditions. There was issue with good intent and bad intent, with respect and disrespect. The guardians of that place had grilled me on who my ancestors were (one of whom is buried on the Flathead Reservation), and on the place and people I currently lived among. They saw I was approaching the wheel in the right way and for the right reasons: I was going as myself, and with the deepest respect for the land and ancestors there; I was not trying to slot into an Indian role or co-opt a tradition. Anyone approaching that kind of power spot in an unbalanced way will either not get there, or experience nothing. It is that simple.

If you work to develop a sacred space, it will more or less operate in the same way: it will grow beyond you and your wishes, and will become its own place that takes position in the larger pattern of the land and will draw or repel people according to their agenda.

Summary

Working magically upon the land often takes on a life of its own; you will find yourself pulled into a pattern and tide that is much bigger than you and that reaches far beyond your time. This is not a bad thing, but it can be a scary thing. Learn how to work on the land, learn how to create gates and work with them. Read the local mythology, the local legends and tales. Learn about the mythical creatures in that area; all of these things will give you clues as to what it is you are working with. Often most stories are heavily overlaid with morals and later added dogmas, but often they have grains of magical truth within them: the key is learning how to separate out what is the pertinent information and what is not.

Keep an open mind and be a curious cat; curiosity and an open mind creates explorers. . . and exploring is the best way to learn magically.

5

Magic and the Land

Part III: Shrines, Land spirits, faeries, deities; having friends around for tea

Part of the work of a magician is the building of shrines. This is done in a variety of ways for lots of different reasons, but the biggest reason is a point of contact and place to exchange energies. How and where you build the shrine depends largely upon what types of beings you are trying to work with, where you are working and why.

If you live in an area that is a strong faery/land spirit area, then it makes sense to work with those beings and use a shrine as a place of exchange. If you are working more in a place where deities are flowing back and forth, then a shrine to work with the local deity would be productive. It also really depends on what work you are trying to achieve.

It is also important to understand that as we change and develop, so the beings we work with and the work we attempt also changes: everything has a time and place and it is useful to be able to bend and flex with that change. So for example you may find yourself working for a span of time with nature/faery beings only to find the work evolving to a point which needs the input of deities or larger powers. There are vast bodies of work however that do not necessitate shrines and such physical level of contact; it is all about using the right tools, the right contacts and the right approach for what it is you are trying to achieve.

Faery/Land Spirit Work

Shrines for land spirits/faery beings are very good bridge builders for friendship and working relationships with the land and the elements.

If you are trying to clean up the land, balance out the impact of civilisation/buildings/pollution, learn about plants and their power, work with animals, and generally learn about the land/beings where you live, then a faery/spirit shrine would be useful. They are also good allies for working with healing, protection, an early warning system and for developing inner sight. The work they ask for is usually simple in human terms and consists of moving things from one place to another, fostering certain plants, cleaning up the land, offering food, and generally being social with them.

In such a case the shrine would be used to make contact, develop a relationship and a place for work. You and the spirits that inhabit or pass through the shrine slowly build up a method of interaction, of energy exchange and eventual friendship.

When working with land spirits/faery beings it is important to understand that they can be unpredictable, do not think the same way that you do and are partial to practical jokes. They anger easily but are also generous when they see clear and good intent. If you are wishing to work with such beings, it pays great dividends to do your homework: find out about the local faery beings through local legends and stories. Research stories and myths of other countries in the same hemisphere as you will find the same stories repeat across many different countries. Many key elements are the same and will teach you operating methods of working with these beings.

Before you start to build the shrine, step out of your normal way of thinking and assess each step in the practical building of the shrine, and think about how it will impact the local environment. This is a very important magical step: think about the construction in terms of the beings that will use it, not yourself and your own satisfaction. For example; shrines are becoming a major fashion at the moment thanks to an interest in Voodoo and similar traditions. People are furiously building shrines and filling them with plastic images, toxic substances and ornaments. If it is in your home, at least you can do no damage. But if you do that out in nature you will get a hostile response or no response at all. Why? Because the materials poison the land, the contents are meaningless/useless to the land spirits and it is more about a grown up playing at 'doll house': you are doing it for your own entertainment and enjoyment rather than to build a working relationship.

Faery/spirit shrines out in nature need to be compatible with nature. They need to be focal points of land energy, for creatures and spirits so the contents need to enhance that, not inhibit or detract from that. So the structure needs to be made of wood or woven sticks, stone, earth; things that are of nature and do not poison the land. Stay away from plastic, nylon etc, anything that is chemical based and does not degrade: the shrine needs to be able to degrade slowly through time as it should not be permanent.

If you wish to work with herbs in the shrine, dried herbs will cut no ice as they have no life left in them, but planting the herbs around the shrine will be well received so long as they are herbs that grow naturally upon that land. Let the weeds grow around them but keep them in check, don't let anything over grow the shrine. I work with a shrine by my house; it is a simple large stone with a flat stone before it that receives the offerings. Flowers and herbs have sprung up around it and the local birds visit it frequently to partake of the offerings.

It is not necessary when trying to attract land/faery spirits to have an image or statue in the shrine; rather it is the reverse (unless it is a deity shrine). Any image or statue can be walked into by a land spirit if the statue is not tuned to a deity (which would only be done if it is a deity shrine) and you may end up with a bit of a problem if you get a bully: once they have a face and a humanesque form to play with it can get a bit tricky. Faery beings are best worked with and are more stable when they are themselves and are not given access to a humanesque interface. It takes longer to learn how to interface with spirits if you have no point of reference like a statue, but perseverance really pays off. Once the spirits have figured out how to communicate with you, the contact becomes much deeper than the type of contact you get when it is filtered through a statue.

Use the shrine to leave food and offerings. Sweet foods like honey, breads, milk, fruit, nuts: you will slowly get a feel for what the spirits like and do not like. The more powerful the substance you leave, the more they can draw on that powerful substance and use it for good or bad. One way to operate is to regularly take out food offerings but where there is some powerful work to be done, then give power substances like coffee, alcohol etc. Just ensure it cannot be accessed by birds or animals and take it away after a day. Do not give power substances on a daily basis; you may end up with a caffeine crazed land spirit that wants to mate with you or move into your house and take over (also a good reason why not to have a faery shrine in the house).

The work would go a little like this: build a shrine out of wood, bark, stones etc, and have a large stone for the beings to reside in. Every day take out food and drink (the local creatures may eat this up, which is not a problem) and sit with the shrine. Talk to the shrine as if the being was there (the action of intent starts an inner calling process) and tell them what you are trying to achieve and why. Do this every day for a full cycle of the moon so that the contact has a chance to build up slowly. After you have been feeding the shrine for a month, on your next visit, sit in silence/meditate in stillness and when you come out of that, take note of what is around you; what creatures are appearing nearby, how does the shrine 'feel', how do you 'feel'? If you have developed your inner senses, just listen to see if anything is trying to reach out to you. If you have problems with such sensitivity, or if it is not normal for you, then you need to develop an inner form of communication which is done in vision using the imagination.

Using vision involves a very simple visionary action: be still and once you are still, use your imagination to see yourself stepping out and standing next to your body. Imagine the shrine before you and look at it through your minds eye; see what looks different, see what seems to shine and what does not. Look at the area around the shrine; see the bushes, trees, water etc around the shrine. If any inner beings have been attracted to the shrine, they will begin to understand that you are using your mind as an interface; they will start to develop ways to contact you through the visionary action as well as dreams and nature cues. At first it will be difficult to tell what is simply your imagination, and what is a real contact. The key to overcoming that is to treat everything as if it were real unless it is very obvious that it is not (like Mickey Mouse appearing or cute butterfly wing faeries).

This will strengthen the interface and stop you second guessing yourself. There will come a cross over point where it becomes very obvious what is real and what is not. You will see something very strange, something you had not expected and you will question yourself. But then you will pick up a book on spirits or local legends, a book that you have not read before, and you will see a description of exactly what you experienced. This is because it is an image interface they have used before with other humans who have then gone on to describe them.

After establishing contact, you will be able to interface with them through vision, dreams and also through instinct and outer happenings. You will notice simple things like a certain bird or creature always appearing when things are getting powerful. The same creature will start to appear in your dreams, or away from the shrine. That is where the contact is starting to strengthen and they are beginning to work with you.

Working at this level with faeries and land spirits is very evocative, imaginative and just plain odd. For a magician who is used to more ordered work and contact it can take some getting used to but it is very rewarding and interesting work. It does have its limits though. Local beings tend to be active only in a certain area and with certain skills. They do not have the reach and power that a land deity would have, but if you are searching for a more 'down to earth' co worker, they are great to work with.

I worked in this way when my children were little and had illnesses. I worked with local land beings, and had a gift area (but not a shrine) where I left things for them and I would sit and talk to them. If my daughter became very sick, I would ask for their help and advice, which would be given. In return they would ask me to plant certain things, move certain things off the land, or pick up trash: all simple stuff for a physical body to do but hard for a spirit to do. They in turn would provide a protective barrier around the children and help their energetic bodies when they were ill. They would also warn me if there was a problem with one of the children, or if there was danger around.

Here is a solid example of shrine work and a not very good way of dealing with it. Unfortunately this was 'retrospective work', i.e. working to re balance a wrong done upon an area of land. A few years ago I was asked to help a family. The grandmother was ill, but the doctors could find no reason for her pain. I went along and found that the old lady had chopped down a bush at the back of the property which had angered some local spirits. This was a wild part of the country (in Montana) where the spirits were strong and still not used to human interaction. They had launched an attack upon her to punish her for cutting down one of their 'houses'.

I managed to negotiate a truce with them. Another bush in the garden would be allowed to grow wild and sweet foods would be placed at the base of the tree every week. They also wanted a gift from her to be buried in the base of the bush. She gave a little medicine wheel she had made and the children buried it for her at the base of the bush. Food was left out and the bush was not touched. Her pains stopped immediately and she started to get better. I called in each week for a month and all was going well.

Six months later I got a call from the family. It had all started up again. I visited the grandmother and she was in pain again. I asked out the routine with the bush and I was told that some flowers had been cut from the bush to put in the house and they had stopped putting out food as they felt it attracted bears. She had broken her agreement. The family asked if I could re negotiate for them. The spirits in the bush were very angry and refused to make any other agreement: the flowers had been cut from the bush, which to them was a crime and the food had stopped which was a breaking of the bond. They felt the family could not be trusted and had not kept up their bargain.

I explained all this to the family. I asked why they had cut flowers from that bush where there was tons of flowers on the other bushes they could have cut with no harm done. The daughter replied that the special bush gave off the best flowers. They did not understand that the best flowers, for whatever reason, were to be protected for the land spirits and were not for humans to touch: that had been the deal - no cutting of the bush in any way.

As for the food, the shrine was far enough away from the house for it to not be a major bear problem and that the bears were all part of the pattern of nature there. Bears came through all the yards in that area anyhow: we were sat right on the edge of the wilderness. I asked if the food had drawn bears into their yard and they said no and admitted they just got lazy and didn't want to go out into the cold to put the food out.

There was nothing I could do. I had set up a way for the humans and spirits to co exist but the humans had not kept up their side of the bargain. Land spirits don't do 'sorry'; if you break a promise then the deal is off. Sad to say the grandmother then suffered pain constantly from that time on and there was nothing anyone could do about it. It was a harsh lesson for her and a major lesson for me also. It taught me a lot about working with land spirits and what they can do, but it also taught me a great deal about personal responsibility and acting as a mediator. You can only set up the conditions, but the people themselves have to keep their side of the bargain and often they would not. They wanted me to fix it again and magic does not work like that; a major component of magic is responsibility and keeping your word.

I felt really bad about walking away knowing that an old lady was in constant pain, but she had to power in her own hands to fix that and chose not to. A harsh lesson was learned by all concerned.

That situation does illustrate how shrines can be used, and the dangers involved when dealing with strong land spirits: always keep your word and keep up your end of the bargain. Land/faery beings will do something for you, but for a price and you must be able and willing to pay that price. Before you agree to do something with a shrine, make sure you can keep up your end of the agreement. If necessary, give a time limit of what you are able to do. Think carefully about what you are willing to undertake and stick to it.

A shrine to land spirits brings the contact into sharp focus which in turn intensifies the contact and the work. This can allow you to achieve and learn a great deal but it is a responsibility that needs thinking about before you undertake it. When I had faery gift areas on my land, I always agreed to uphold it for as long as I lived in that place, and when I moved on I would stop working with it. That was part of the agreement I made. It's just a matter of stating your boundaries and them stating theirs.

Deity Shrines

Working with deities on the land can be very powerful and a good source of great learning. There are two main ways to approach it; one is to work with a known deity and the other is to reach out to a deity that is still within or upon the land but has fallen into obscurity.

Working with a known deity involves a bit of background research; it is important to know if that deity is compatible with the land and community, and to know what the power is that the deity mediates. In some countries like the UK, deities were brought in from other countries to protect and assist invaders, immigrants etc: some blended well and some did not. It is wise to question your own motives in setting up work with a specific deity: is it because you wish to work with and learn from a particular power or are you simply following a current 'occult fashion'?

Working with a deity that is not directly involved with nature is pointless in an outside shrine. For example Athena, a goddess who was very fashionable for a time is a power that works in temples, in cities and with male warriors. It is pointless having a nature shrine out in the countryside and putting a city connected goddess in there. Whereas a deity connected to creatures or the fertility of the land would be ideal.

Are you wishing to work with a deity or worship them? If it is the latter, then it is better to work within a religious setting rather than a purely magical one. I work with deities magically but not religiously, so my techniques will not be best for someone wishing to become a devotee of a particular deity. There is a clear distinction between the two approaches and they have very different outcomes.

Known Deity Shrines

If you are wishing to build a shrine to a deity out on the land, first make sure they would be happy to be worked with out on the land. Ensure that the land spirits would be compatible with the deity so that you do not inadvertently create conflict in an area.

It pays great dividends to carefully choose the correct deity and if the god or goddess is from another land, use vision or readings to see how your land would react to them. It is also a good idea to see what elements or powers would balance the deity so that you do not end up working with a lopsided power. If you research well, which is easy these days with the internet, look into what companions, what tools and what spirits are depicted with a particular deity and instead of just working with text, allow your instincts to also contribute. It can be a very interesting learning experience.

The first step, once the deity is chosen (or they have chosen you) is to build the outer shrine on a chosen patch of land like in a garden/ yard etc. Again care needs to be taken in what materials you use to ensure that you do not put the local wildlife or land at risk. Natural materials are good, bits of plastic are bad.

Take care to build in accordance to what the deity needs and the tools you wish to work with, as opposed to building in a way that simply looks good: a shrine is not a New Age display, it is a working space and needs to be constructed with that in mind. Once the construct is in place, introduce the image of the deity to the shrine so that the interface is ready for activation.

The next step is the inner opening of the shrine. This work is done in vision and allows the inner flow of power across the land to integrate with the shrine and allow the intermediary powers of the deity to flow into the image. A simple way of doing this is to sit before the shrine and still yourself. Using meditation, still yourself until your mind has settled and slowly become aware of your surroundings in vision. With eyes closed, see the space around you and see yourself walking around the land space. You may notice that your home or building does not appear upon the land, which is normal if it is a modern building. Buildings, unless they are consecrated spaces or temples, tend to take hundreds of years to fully appear in the inner landscape of the land.

When you have a clear vision of the land around you, slowly imagine the shrine building up upon the land until it clearly appears on the inner landscape. It may take more than one session to build the inner image strongly enough for it to stay. Notice with the building of the shrine, it is done only through physical construction and then imaginary imprint, which is very different from constructing a temple which involves many different beings and working with visionary magical construction. Building a shrine is akin to setting up a telephone line to a deity as opposed to a fully constructed workspace like a temple.

When the shrine is clear in your mind on the inner landscape, then it is time to 'open the doors' to call the deity in. Sometimes this happens naturally with shrines and the deity power will almost immediately begin communicating with you. Other times you need to open the door. This is done by lighting a candle in front of or within the shrine (when it is windy, putting a tea light in a glass jar works well), and working the shrine like an altar. 'Se' the flame with your inner vision and see the shrine as a gateway. Using inner vision, call through the gateway for a priest or priestess of the deity to work with you as an inner contact to activate and guide you in the work of the shrine. A figure will be drawn to the shrine and will appear to you in vision: talk with them, ask them to work with you and guide you.

That is all that is needed from a visionary magic point of view. The key is to try and maintain contact with the priest or priestess in a way that works best for you, either through vision, dreams or instinct. The inner contact will act as a slow door opener and mediator for the deity power to flow into the shrine, a bit like an interpreter. Working regularly with the shrine, working with it as an altar and a place of offerings will slowly open the door wider and allow a natural interaction to develop.

Take note of how the animals, birds and plants respond to the shrine: if the power is unbalanced, it will negatively affect the wildlife around it. If it is positive, you will notice that plants flourish, more birds visit and the wildlife becomes more noticeable. The shrine becomes a working point of focus and can be used for all manner of nature work in conjunction with the deity. Often they take on a life of their own and teach you how to work with and for them.

Local Deities and Ancient Powers

The actual construction method of the shrine would be the same as the method above, but the chances are there are no available images of the local deity as most ancient gods and goddesses in Europe, for example, were overlaid and forgotten. If that is the case then your detective work has to be mainly in vision.

Taking your time to work in vision by repeatedly walking through the inner landscape will enable you to connect with any ancient deities that are still accessible upon or within the land. For example in one place where I lived, I wanted to know who and what the local deity powers were. I lit a candle, sat down and went in vision, seeing myself walking out of my house, down the road and into the fields and the forest. I did this a few times and slowly got used to the land I had moved to. I also became aware of local spirits, ancestors and a large burial mound with guardians that appeared in the inner landscape but not in the outer landscape. There was no burial mound anywhere near where I was living that I was aware of.

The next time I went in vision, I talked to the guardians who told me the Mother of that land was sleeping in the mound and had been trapped there for a very long time by human magic from another land. I went to the doorway of the mound that the guardians showed me and the door had a crucifix upon it and behind that, lots of script and strange looking symbols. The guardians told me that people had locked the goddess in the mound a long time ago and although they still guarded her, they could not set her free; only a human could undo what a human had done.

I decided to take the job on and spent time repeatedly going in vision to clear things off the door before slowly dismantling the door/blockage step by step. Eventually I managed to get the door open and go inside. A goddess was sleeping on the ground, surrounded by black dogs. One of the dogs woke up and barked, which woke her up. She was very angry, not at being woken, but at humans magically sealing her into the mound.

I apologised for how she had been treated in the past and I agreed to help her leave, which in retrospect was not such a good idea. She was angry, very angry and she wanted revenge. It took a lot of negotiating to calm her down and one of the negotiations included a shrine, offerings and adjustments to the surrounding land and to how I lived upon the land. She is essentially a warrior goddess, specific to a small area, essentially the village and surrounding land, and she has a very fixed idea as to how humans should interact with her.

These local deities can be very difficult to work with and they seem to be a combination of deity, ancestral consciousness and land spirits. After my experience with this goddess, I tend these days to be very wary of this level of deity as they are so unpredictable and difficult to work with. But such work is not impossible if you work with a bit more care than I did, and find out a lot more about the local deities before interacting with them. In retrospect I should have consulted with local ancestors, inner contacts and land spirits to learn more about the deity power before deciding to hack down a magical barrier. That way, I would have been better prepared to interact with her and would be better able to counter any danger posed by opening an ancient contact of power.

If you do decide to build a shrine to a local deity, keep it simple and use it as a point of contact and offerings. The more you work it the more they will get the idea that it is a place to meet and work, and they will keep their interactions with you confined to the shrine: there is nothing worse than having a local spirit/ancestor/deity tramping through your home at all hours of the day and night. Which also brings me to another point. This method of building a shrine outside can also be used as a meeting place of contact for local ancestors: essentially a shrine is a magical meeting point for you to connect with local spirits/beings. It is the intent that counts and the slow building both in vision and ritual of action/intent that will tune the shrine into focus.

When you have come to the end of working with a shrine, or you are going to move, bury any deity image (unless you are taking it with you), break up the shrine and let it go back into nature. Leave a last gift and tell the spirits that you are going, why you are going and where you are going to. If they are long range beings, they may be waiting for you in your new home, whether you like it or not. Putting down boundaries at the very beginning of the relationship (I will only work with you here) can be a good idea!

Befriending Local Spirits/Ancestors and Having Them Live With You

This is an interesting way of working should you cross paths with local ancestors in the area where you live. If you live in a city, you are more likely to get confused ghosts that find you (magic switches all the lights on and draws them in) and seek refuge with you. In such instance they will either want help passing into and through death, or they will want a place to hide and rest.

If you do end up with a resident ghost that is not ready to move on, then living with them can be simple: just state your boundaries and give them a safe corner of the house to 'reside' in. As long as they do not cause problems and do not drain energy from you (in which case a parasite is masquerading through a ghost shell), then they will live happily in an area of the house and will leave when they are ready.

Under these circumstances it is not a good idea to work magically with them or interact too much: remember this is a stranger who is unbalanced or needy and giving them shelter is enough. Much more than that can cause problems for the living and the dead. Often they will suddenly vanish during a magical working: the gates open and they are pulled through into death.

When my cousin died after a long and terrible illness, he hung out with my partner and I for a while. He would not cause problems other than blowing the light bulbs on a near daily basis: he was terrified of death and in his terror he latched on to our home and hid there. Slowly he began to relax as he realised that he still 'existed' and I was not going to attempt to move him on. Coming to the understanding of their new state and form of existence is a major shift of awareness, and if they can make that shift themselves it becomes a major part of their learning and evolution as a soul. So let them have some time to get used to the idea.

After a while, we were due to go and work with a magical group in Bath so off we went, and my cousin came too. He sat in the back of the car, which felt a bit odd, came with us to the working and sat in a chair as we opened the gates. He sat through a couple of the magical workings and was picked up on by one of the magicians ("I can smell alcohol", said one worker – my cousin was an alcoholic). The major working of the day was underway and suddenly he just vanished through the gates. That was it. He had overcome his fear, seen where he was supposed to be and not supposed to be, and had moved on of his own accord with his own understanding.

This is a bit different to moving into a house that has a resident ghost, which is usually someone who is trapped, or a parasite, or an echo. Those must be dealt with in a specific way (see my book; *The Exorcist's Handbook*)

A very different type of ancestral work is where you cross paths with an ancient ancestor who is purposely staying in our world for a specific reason. They will find you, often through very strange routes, and it tends to happen more frequently out in the country where there is less 'civilised psychic noise'. Because we know so little of the culture and beliefs of our ancient ancestors you really have to play it by ear.

As I have discussed in my books before, when I move into an area, I go to the local burial ground ·or cemetery and make friends with the people buried there: I show respect and honour those who have lived upon the land before me. Often that is enough but on one occasion something very interesting happened.

I slowly began to make friends in the local village where I was living and my neighbour began to understand that I was a little bit, well, odd. Her family had lived in that area as farmers for at least a 1,000 years that they knew of and were very closely connected to the land. One day she came to me with a bundle and sat down to tell me a story about her grandfather. He was a local farmer and had begun to expand his farm decades ago, by ploughing rough land that they owned but had never touched.

The ploughing dug up a body, an old skeleton from one of the mounds in the rough field. His friend who was a doctor looked at the body and said it was very old, not a recent one. The grandfather took the skull, which was the best preserved part of the remains, and gave it a home in his house, where it lived quietly in the corner for decades. When he and then his son died, his granddaughter was clearing the house out and came across the skull; she remembered the story of it from when she was a little girl. She did not want to throw it away or pass it on to historians who would not respect it. So she brought it to me, after having a strong instinct that I would look after it.

   After she left, I placed the skull on the table and tentatively felt around it for any presence. Many remains do not have any connection to their original owners, but some do. I was also very aware of something my first teacher told me, which was that when you work magic, things happen for a reason, things find their way to you for a reason and one must find out what that reason is. She was very clear about this and saw reason in everything. I was not that convinced and I still feel it is important to differentiate between every day happenings and magical jobs/events: but never take anything for granted either way.

   So I felt around the skull and yes, there was a faint something, like a whisper. I went into vision with my hands on the skull and came across a young girl, very young, maybe 12 or 13yrs old. She was very strong, very present and was showing me birds. She tried to convey to me that she worked with birds, in what we would call a magical way, though to her it was normal. I told her I too had worked with birds and she nodded, saying that was why she wanted to come and live with me.

   I questioned myself: I was not sure how much of this was just my own imagination as it was a slightly different way of working to what I am used to and I was on uncertain ground. I found her a place in the house to live; on a shelf with my birds, feathers etc that I had collected. She seemed happy enough.

Over time I began to learn a lot from her about local birds, how to call them in, how to 'fly' with them in my mind and also how the local winds worked. A friend came to visit me who is an archaeologist and he took a look at the skull. Without doing tests he said it was difficult to confirm, but his opinion was a child aged somewhere between 12 to 14 and it was very old. Hmmm.

So I worked with her for a couple of years and then one day she wanted to go to sleep. I did not quite understand what she meant and it took me a week or two to figure it out. In the meantime she was getting frustrated and was beginning to get disruptive. Things were flying off the shelf, birds were hitting the window or pecking at the window; it was the inner worlds trying to shout for attention.

Eventually I figured it out and got her a casket. I put the skull in the casket and did a reading to find out where she wanted to be buried. She did not want burying, but she wanted to sleep where I slept. So she was moved into the bedroom, still in her casket, and was placed beneath a bit of furniture so she was hidden. She sleeps for certain lengths of time but occasionally she will awaken and will ask to be back out among the living for a period of time.

I do not know why she does not want burying, or even how her spirit had managed to hold on to the skull for so long. It is all part of an ongoing learning experience for me and we are in such a magical dark age that we need to find our own way through the dark and figure it out as we go along.

I have learned a great deal from her and she has found sanctuary, a good trade! I began to think about how magicians use skulls, often without respect and without care for who the skull belonged to; there seems to be little emphasis on trying to find out if the skull is still connected to a spirit and what that spirit may need. It has become a fashion to have a skull, along with a glamorous grimoire, etc and it makes me wonder what effect this is having on the magicians and the ancestors that are still connected to the skulls.

I certainly learned to be far more conscious and compassionate towards body remains, and learned that there is a lot more to working with skulls than meets the eye: sometimes those skulls might not want to work, they may want to sleep.

So if some remains come your way, particularly unexpectedly, and you are a magician, step back before including the skull in your work; take the time to try and find out who they are and what they need; why did they come to you? Find out what you can do for them before asking what they can do for you.

Summary

Working with the land and the powers that flow through the land is ideally a natural, instinctive interaction with everything around you: no dressing, no shrines, just you and nature. That works immediately for some and not for others. For those who find such formless work a bit overwhelming or difficult to penetrate, then working with shrines, offering areas and key places upon the land is an intermediary step towards building up a relationship with the powers around you.

I still work with an outside offering area that houses a large stone, not only to keep in touch with the land beings, but to also feed the birds and creatures in winter. Building up a relationship with the land involves connecting to the land spirits, deity powers and also the local creatures, birds, waterways, springs, hills and rocks.

Differentiating between temple based deities usually with heavily formed rituals, and land spirits/ancient deities of nature is important: know who you are working with and why. Temple based deities work best with you through temple spaces, altars and other interfaces. Nature deities connect with you through the elements, the creatures, and the land. They connect directly with you and they can certainly pack a punch!

Working in such a way is an interesting and good training exercise for a magician: we can get too locked into a system and end up shutting out all of the powers around us. It is better to learn different ways of working, different types of contacts etc as it is all part of the bigger picture and creates a well rounded magician. We are in a culture of specialisation and magic can get sucked into that mentality too.

Learn the basic structures through one path, then branch out and learn in as many directions as possible so that you gain experience and also allow for the right skill set to find you. After many years you will find that you naturally start to specialise, once you have learned many different skills. That specialisation 'wires' you to a focus point so that you become 'adept' in a certain area. But specialising too much too quickly has the opposite effect. Let it happen naturally and in the meantime, if you are a heavily ritualised magician, get out on the land. If you are more shamanic in your practice, learn how to work within a temple setting. The learning never stops!

6

Working with the Magical Elements

Knowing which way is up

In Western magic we work with the directions and the elements as an integral part of our magical practice. This manifests itself in the use of direction altars, magical tools connected to elements (sword, wand, cup and shield/stone) and the elements placed with the directions; east/air, south/fire, west/water, north/earth. There are some variants of this within certain traditions but on the whole a consistent pattern runs through Western magic. It also pops up in various religions in a number of ways and when you recognise this, it helps you to see what the 'builders' of that religion or magical tradition were reaching for.

When looking at the magical elements and directions in tradition, there are two things to be aware of. The first is that some recently formed traditions have aligned their use of the magical directions in accordance with psychology and poetic expression. That is more relevant for a religious pattern, like Wicca for example, but not so useful for magic, particularly magic that reaches deep into the inner worlds. The psychologised use of the directions and elements works only to the threshold of the human psyche and not beyond and is therefore limited in deeper magic.

The second is that some magical/Pagan traditions developed their use of the magical directions in direct relationship to the land they were on. This is a layer of magic that works directly with the land upon which you are stood and the beings that inhabit that land. When those traditions are moved to a different land, it is important to be aware that more surface directional patterns may not work. So for example some Western Mystery paths work with mountains in the north, sea in the west etc. That is not going to work in a lot of places. If you are working in conjunction with the land and the beings that inhabit that land, then you have to go back to the drawing board and work with what is actually there upon the land.

Some directional powers go much deeper than the land and are not about the physical direction but the magical direction. The magical direction is where the power of a particular element has been worked with over millennia and formed through a certain orientation, a certain group of deities and has been developed through a temple or ritual system. They can be worked with in ritual and vision on many different levels from basic workings, to conditional magical group workings and beyond.

The ultimate expression of power that flows out of the magical direction gives the magician a connection to the deepest and most beautiful patterns of creation and destruction; the universe in action. At this level, the power cannot be controlled and any attempt to control and over form the power will cause it to degenerate before it shuts down and withdraws. The deepest expression of power that flows from the magical directions is there to be experienced and mediated, often without form and most certainly without and beyond human understanding. You become a part of something much bigger than yourself and by engaging in such powerful service, the power flows through you, changing you as it flows out into the world. You undergo personal change without focus on the self, but with focus on service, on a selfless act.

To get to that level of work takes time and much learning. It is best to start at the bottom of the ladder and work up. Learn how the elemental directions and powers work, learn how the contacts of each direction work, learn about the magical tools, about how the conditional form of power works as it flows from the inner realm to the outer world. Learn about the magical structures, inner temples, and inner realms accessed through the thresholds of east, south, west and north. Learn about how the elements of air, fire, water and earth can be worked with magically and once you have pulled all those threads of learning together, then it is time to throw all the structure away and stand in the midst of power. Only by learning the form can you step beyond it: one must learn the outer forms of magic, and work within those structures to gain knowledge and experience, to develop a working practice and most importantly to prepare the mind and body for the greater levels of power that come with deeper work.

Once you can work at a level beyond the appearance of the structures i.e. the temples, beings, tools etc, then you can really begin to mediate the true elemental powers that flow through and out of the elemental directions. When you have reached that stage of connection with the raw powers, then the force and nature of those powers truly begin to affect change in your body, mind and soul.

The outer magical actions that a magician learns through training triggers the process of change within the magician, first through opening our awareness of the wider inner worlds and of consciousness. We begin to learn about ourselves and about the worlds that we inhabit beyond the physical realm. The development comes slowly, through practical learning and by observing the action/reaction process in magic that affects everything around us. If you are truly open to learning, then the first stages of training, i.e. ritual, astrology, patterns, vision, Tarot etc will act as a ballast and awakening of the consciousness. Working in vision with inner contacts moves the magician a step further and begins to reveal the dynamics of action, the wider affects, the consequences and connections between the magician and their actions. It also takes the magician's ego down a peg or two when the realisation comes that we are but a small link in a very large chain of consciousness.

The deeper gifts of self-empowerment, development and maturation that we seek through magic begin to develop through our actions and reactions to the power: we develop as a result of the mediation and its affect upon our bodies and our outer lives. The power will fill whatever is happening in our daily lives and will confront us with a deeper gnosis of the nature of events that challenge us as we grow and mature.

The power will also fill our bodies, finding the consciousness in our organs and interacting at a deep level to bring about change. How that change will manifest in our bodies depends upon how we let go and allow that change to happen, and how we consciously interact with both the power and the spirits that reside as mediators within our organs. We are made up of many different forms of consciousness and working with the elemental powers that interact with those forms of consciousness brings about change and regeneration.

The following section breaks down some of the details about the directions, the elements and the deeper contacts within the directions. *Magical Knowledge I* section 2 chapter 2 (page 120 onwards) presents details regarding the magical tools and the basic working practice to open the elemental four directions to make contacts, so I will not repeat them here. It is important to learn about these factors in magic not just by reading about them, but by actually practicing, experimenting and engaging with the powers to do active work.

The Powers and Qualities
of the Elemental Directions

East: Element of Air, powers of justice, the sword/blade, warrior virgin goddesses/gods, sacred utterance, sacred alphabets, sacred writings, knowledge keepers, sigil formation, working with the weather, the whirlwind.

South: Element of Fire, powers of healing and poisons/disease, the wand/staff, solar deities and the power of the Sun, The Golden City, kingships, war/cleansing by fire, volcanic magic, firestorm.

West: Element of Water, powers of generation/genetics/humanity, the cup/chalice/cauldron, deities of the sea, rivers, wells, midwife of life and death, divination, the second sight, the threshold of death, the ocean.

North: Element of Earth, depths of death and the dawn of regeneration, the shield, the Underworld/Dark Goddess, Earth Goddess, the Abyss, Divinity within substance, the stone/mountain/cave.

Centre: the void; a state of potential where there is stillness and silence: the intake of breath before the universe is breathed out into existence.

To truly begin working in the four directions, an element of practice is needed so that you familiarize yourself with the energetic feel of each threshold; this is far more important than memorizing attributes. It is better to go out in the garden and experience the flowers in real life than it is to sit in a house and learn the flowers names, colours and smells.

The directions have many layers and depths to them, and bear in mind that the information is this chapter is just one perception, one understanding. The directions do not really change according to belief structures — they are what they are — but how each culture perceives them and approaches them is very different.

It is also important to understand that they differ according to how you approach them: the layers reveal themselves to you depending upon what your focus of intent is. To approach this type of work from a point of view such as wishing to connect with the elemental/ natural powers, that will give you a different experience from intending to approach the directions from the point of view of the inner priest/ priestesshoods which would take you to the thresholds of the Inner temples.

Intending to connect with the powers of Divinity with this form of magic will give you a different experience again. It is all down to frequencies and therefore intent: the more you work in the directions with the elements, the more aware you will become of the different levels, frequencies and vibrations that the elements/powers express themselves through. The different levels manifest for us as different presentations from deep vision, to inner contact, and to outer enlivened tools.

What method you use will also give you a very different experience. The main two methods used in magic are ceremonial (ritual) and visionary. In ritual you bring the powers of the elements, deities and inner contacts into your physical world by way of a pattern, an utterance and the use of sigils. The power can be tied into substance and used. Ceremony can also open doors for powers to pass through and the conditional extent of the ritual will decide what that power will do.

Most magicians get themselves into messes at one point or other in their ceremonial lives through the conditional manifestation of power. But there are many safeguards in place to stop the novice from treading where they shouldn't. The biggest safeguard is if you don't know what you are doing from an inner point of view in such work, then the outer pattern either will not work or it will only trigger a minor effect.

Here is a breakdown of the directional elements in more depth;

East:
The Power of Utterance and Swords

If ever a magical direction was a reflection of an epoch of humanity, I would say that the age we are currently living in is the age of the east. I say east in a magical sense, not a topographical sense. Yes you would work magically with the power of the east at an east facing altar, but that is just a surface land expression; the power of the east is so much more than that as a magical direction. The magical east is a threshold for a specific quality of power that flows into our world and its element is air. Let's look at some of the manifestations of this power that flows out of the magical east and how we can work with it.

Utterance

The use of utterance, the use of the voice and the breath is the most basic and powerful form of magic that flows from the magical east.

Everything else flows from that basic expression, that bridging of a magical power that we breathe in, convert and then mediate out as a magical pattern. The use of breath was and is the most fundamental magical tool we have at our disposal. Curses, bindings, blessings, invocations, calling the wind, breathing the weather, bridging sacred utterance into substance; the list is endless. These are uses of the element of air that we see in most religions today, and in all magical paths.

There are two basic principles that work with the power of utterance, one is contacted/mediated utterance and the other is un-contacted utterance within a pre existing power pattern. Contacted utterance is where the magician acts as a bridge between an inner world consciousness and the outer world. This can mean anything from releasing a wind power from the inner worlds out into the air (weather working), reciting a magical pattern/chant/tone that is a sound which brings about magical change such as a contacted ritual, to breathing life into substance.

The un-contacted utterance is the recital of words or songs/chants that were originally mediated from inner to outer, and are learned rote fashion to be recited or performed at key times of the year or within specific conditions. The use of the exact same words in the exact same way triggers the original magical ritual/intent that brought about the creation of the song/chant/recitation. So for example, in the Catholic Mass, the recitation of the mass unchanged in Latin over centuries created a ritual pattern that power could flow through. If you change the pattern drastically, it no longer mediates the power and becomes meaningless.

Songs and chants are interesting ones. Sound frequencies and pitch have a very interesting effect on substance and energy. Depending on whether it is a high pitch or low pitch, it will repel or attract certain orders of beings. The use of bells, gongs, horns and cymbals etc in sacred chant and music is a part of this use of sound to affect substance. Certain recitations and songs, when constructed ritually, affect the substance of the building and the land upon which it stands over time; hence the use in so many religions and magical traditions. Often it is not the actual words, but the pitch, frequency and rhythm that affect the change. Saying that, in certain languages that are used magically/religiously as well as for every day communication, for example Hebrew, the use of specific letters and words do have particular magical effect.

For the longest time I did not buy into this concept of a letter and word being a sacred expression within itself, simply because I had no direct experience of it. I tend to be a major sceptic until proven otherwise. But then I was taught about the sacred use of letters, utterances and words, and I began to work with them. And work they did, in the most powerful and extraordinary way.

The use of breath to mediate the utterance of Divinity/the breath of life is a major element of magic, and can be the deepest magical act anyone can ever do. Methods for working with this power in magical forms are discussed in my book *Magical Knowledge III*.

To experiment practically with this concept, the best way to work is not in script or already formed patterns of ritual, but to stand at the altar of the east and work in vision and ritual at the same time. Work in vision with a specific contact that mediates the power of utterance while also mediating that power through ritual, speech, breathing out of power, and directing it or writing at the altar.

It is one of those things that you need to play around with to see what form of mediation you are best able to perform. For me it was simply breathing out while bridging the power. That breath was either released out into the world, or it was placed within substance to enliven it.

South:
The Power of the Sun and Fire

Fire is the other magical element that is still used widely in magic and religious mystical practice. This can express itself from the simple use of a candle flame to tune in a direction or power, to using the power of the black sun to destroy a nation. In between, thankfully, there are many stages of fire/solar power that can be worked with in various ways, some of which I have mentioned in other books and therefore do not need to repeat here. These are some of the things not covered in the other books.

Fires:
Sending Power (Curses, Seething)

Flames, such as candle flames and fires can be used to move power from A to B. Such action can be done by working with focussed intent and ritual action, or by utterance. What you do and how you do it will largely depend upon what you are trying to achieve.

The use of a candle flame to dispatch patterns of magic is a useful tool, for example in the case of a Kabbalistic curse or highly patterned ritual attack. When such an attack is ritually constructed, it acquires a specific pattern/shape that can be seen from an inner visionary point of view. Even if the attack was constructed using lettering, sigils, utterance etc, it will still have an inner shape expression which appears to us as a 3D pattern.

If it cannot be dismantled using visionary techniques for whatever reason, and it is not a major construction, then it can be dispatched and dismantled using a candle flame. This method requires a highly developed mental focus, one of the pre requisites of more powerful magic. The basic technique is to light the flame and then focus upon the flame. Imagine the shape of the pattern appearing in the flame; capture the 'feeling' of the pattern, and your body's awareness of the pattern (each attack has a specific 'feel' to it). Let that image and awareness build in the flame until it is stable and once you can hold that image in the flame, utter your intent into the flame ('I reject you and cast you into the void', for example) and blow the flame out with the intent that your breath sends it to wherever you are directing it. The action often has to be repeated in intervals over a few days to break the pattern down.

That method is very effective with certain levels of magic, though it will not address really nasty well crafted attacks. It can be used to construct and magically send things in both positive and negative ways but regardless of the good or bad intent behind it, if you are instigating an action, rather than responding to an action, you must be fully aware of the unfolding of the pattern, its affect upon you, whether it draws power from you etc before you act. Often magicians throw power around in anger, rage, depression etc and it is an infantile thing to do. It is also a self-defeating act: initiating a magical act that directly and conditionally affects another human being will place you in an energetic relationship with that person. That can take a lot of getting out of and ends up being more bother than it is worth. It's the old cause and effect seesaw again.

However, when in a hostile situation and magic has been thrown at you, sticking it in the flame and putting it in the void does not affect you, but it does drain the sender: all of their hard work and energy is flowing down a dark hole.

Another way of using fire ritually in the south is to build a large fire and ritually build up power around it. When the power is at breaking point, the intent is cast into the fire. This is usually a more emotive way of working, rather than the controlled focussed way of working. It is seen most often in folk magic but is very potent in its effects. For this reason, it is important for the magician to be aware of it and its effects, so that if you are confronted with it, you will know what it is, how it works and what to do with it.

Where I grew up in Yorkshire, this folk method was known as 'seething'; probably a lap over from our Viking past. It was not viewed as a specific thing that was done, rather a woman (it was usually women) who was enraged at a person's actions, would build up her anger and stand before the fire shouting and uttering curses into the fire, with the curses aimed at a specific person. The woman would be full of rage, would often shake with rage, would sometimes cut a finger and cast blood into the fire as they cursed. Whether or not this is directly connected to the Nordic tradition of seething I don't know, but the area I grew up had a rich Viking past.

I have been around a woman seething, and I tell you, I would not want to be on the receiving end of that. It's feral, powerful and destructive. But if someone is on the receiving end of it, then directing that power from them back into a fire (same idea as the candle flame method) and into the void (rather than back to the person who sent it) is a good way of disengaging from it. The reason it is not sent back to the person is because with such action you end up in a game of magical ping pong where power is thrown back and forth until someone buckles. Best just to stick it in the void and let them wear themselves out.

Working with the Sun Temple

The contacts in the south come from a variety of different lines, the most commonly worked one being the 'Sun Temple'. This is a generic or 'root' contact from which flows the many solar based religions around the world. Their work is tied in with civilisations, empires, kingships, and when it is in balance, it is a powerful but

compassionate force that flows through great nations. When it is out of balance, it mediates greed, lust for power, battles for resources, supremacy and blood lust.

In a magical setting, the power of the sun is formed and mediated into patterns that we interact with in the form of priesthoods that work with fate. Often this appears in myths and ancient stories as a board game where the fate of nations, family lines and individuals is manipulated to bring about change. These powers do not create fate or oversee fate, rather they change and interfere with fate. The best way to learn about these priesthood lines is to work in vision at the altar in the south before the flames or before a large fire, and reach for an inner contact of that line.

The deeper aspect of the solar power in the south is the power of fire in the pattern of creation on the Tree of Life. Part of the element of the angelic patterning for creation is fire and it is an inner power that brings light and life to the pattern/ritual that is being worked. Learning to work with fire in vision for example, in the desert of the Tree of Life will teach you all you need to know about how fire works in magic. Working with the fire, communing with it, interacting with it, and learning how to work with the angelic beings that oversee that element teaches the magician a great deal. You would not work with a 'named' angel, rather you would reach into fire in vision to find the angelic contact that is the mediator of that power.

West: The Power of Genetics and Water

Working in the west is also referred to as working in the Sea Temple. Many beginner magical books will simply say the cup is in the west and it represents love etc. But the west is so much more than that and people forget to look beyond the beginner presentation: they do not realise it is less than 1% of what is actually there.

The west is primarily about life and death, waves of generations (genetics), waves of humanity, other species and blood lines. It is about vessels that contain power, whether that power is to regenerate or kill. It is also the home of the moon, of creativity, insanity and visions.

Approaching work in the magical west can take a few different forms. One form that is worked with is the Sea Temple that I mentioned earlier. This can be approached in a number of ways, either working directly in vision with the sea or reaching this ancient temple via the Great Library. There is no ritual way of working with the Sea Temple that I am currently aware of, other than very nature based, almost 'shamanic' ways of working at the sea edge with cup/blood etc. It is a very vision orientated direction and because it does not have an outer temple manifestation in our world, vision is the best way to work with it (for example we still have temples to Ra, the Sun God in Egypt, so that outer manifestation can be worked with ritually).

Working in the Sea Temple would focus mainly upon global weather or the blood line of races. The deep sea is where our weather comes from so if a magician wanted to be of service to the climate, for example, she would work in the Sea Temple to help restore balance. The work would be done in vision and would be unconditional; when working with something as powerful as the climate, you have to be really careful to not try and consciously 'fix' the climate.

There are two reasons for that: one is that if you work in this deep temple with a fixed agenda, then you will be working alone and will achieve nothing; it would be like a gnat pissing in the wind. The second reason is that our limited understanding of the weather would drive us to calm the weather down, which is maybe not what it actually needs. The weather has its own way of rebalancing itself and we need to just add energy to that process.

If you approach the Sea Temple with an unconditional willingness to work, then you will be working with vast numbers of contacts, adding your small fraction of work as a contribution. We as a species have caused so much damage, therefore we must give of our strength and power to assist in the rebalancing of all that. The best way to do that as magicians is to turn up in the deep Sea Temple and offer to help. You will be put to work but you most likely will have no clue as to what you are doing or why. And you don't need to.

Springs and fresh water

Working with fresh water is another way of working with the magical west. Not only are springs about healing or guarding the land, they also carry information through the land both on the surface and underground. Working ritually at the west altar with water and then replacing it back into the rivers or waterways can be a very powerful way of working. Again because the power of water is so vast and beyond our understanding, it is best to work in an unconditional way that changes the water for whatever is needed for the land and the springs.

Water also holds memory, it holds information, and this quality can also be used to mediate magical knowledge from the Great Library or the inner temples to the outer world in order for it to be there for people in the future. The information is carried out of the inner worlds, mediated into the water which is then poured into the rivers. The knowledge will stay within the water, wherever the water goes, and any magician in the future who is capable of extracting that information will be able to work with it.

The Vessel

Working magically with cups can be very interesting work. Not only are they containers but they are also mediators. Using a cup or vessel in ritual can act by containing the power worked on and the water/wine/blood that is held within the cup is used to mediate the power. It is the cup, not the fluid which is the doorway to the power: the water simply carries the power of the cup. The cup can be used empty as a mediator of power from the west. So for example if there is an imbalance of power, for instance too much fire power coming through, placing the magical cup within the midst of that power will moderate it.

This is where you begin to learn how the different directions work together to off set the pure power of each other. You can see some of this co-operation and modifying power working between the directions in myths and legends. Swords placed in stones, swords in relation to cups, fire over water etc.

Working in ritual with the cup/vessel teaches the magician the mechanism of how substance can hold power, how the shaping of the substance dictates its ability to hold power and how that power can affect the elements which in turn affects magic. The vessel can also hold fire, which is another old combination with the west: the fires of Brigh who is a goddess of springs, warriors, smith-craft etc. A magical fire in a consecrated cauldron will allow the magician to work with modified fire, fire that is contained within a vessel that holds the inner power of water.

This modified power can work on shaping and forging the magician and bringing magical patterns into form safely. This is also the direction and magical tool of the alchemist; this is where the transmutation of substance, the enlivening of inert substance and the marriage of elements all comes together to create something new and wonderful.

North: The Power of Earth, Rock

The north as an elemental magical direction is probably the oldest magical direction because it is the threshold that takes us back to our early ancestors and the very first temples (that we know of) that were developed in the Mesolithic era.

It is an interesting and often widely misunderstood direction and similarly the element of earth is also widely misunderstood in magic. It is taken as simply a shield, a protection when it is far more than that. This magical direction is where the magician would learn about the depths of death, the Underworld, ancient sleepers, faery beings, and very early ancestors. The magician would learn to work with rock, earth, sand etc in magical construction, i.e. golem making, worked with in conjunction with the east (utterance). The north also teaches the magician about disease, destruction, sending consciousness through substance and how to work with mountains and fault lines via caves deep within the Earth.

The Underworld and Abyss

Using the north temple of earth as an access point, we can gain entry into the ancient Underworld temples that were scattered around the world in our distant past. By doing so we can learn about the destroying powers of certain deities, Sekhmet for example, how they operate and why. We can also reach deep into the Underworld, where very old deities sleep and access their ancient temples in order to learn about the powers they wielded, their function in the surface world and what led them to retire deep into the land.

Those sleeping ancients eventually pass into the Abyss as they become far removed from our consciousness, and for a short while, we can access them as they sleep in their tunnel/cave in the Abyss while it still has a doorway from the Underworld to the Abyss. Eventually that Underworld doorway is closed and sealed over time, so that there is no way to reach a very ancient being other than to go down the Abyss.

The Abyss can be reached by working in the vision of the desert (Tree of Life) and standing at the edge of the Abyss: the magician asks the guardian of the Abyss to allow her access, or the magician can access the Abyss via very old Underworld temples that still have unsealed doors. Such action can be a strain upon the body as the magician must work deep in vision to reach the depths of such a place. The Abyss is where powers that no longer have a place in our world go to sleep until the world is no longer manifest. Then they will release and return to source. You can reach some of these ancient powers to work with them, but you would have to have a very good reason, as the impact to the magician's body is a high price to pay.

It is better to work within the Underworld temples if you can as they are less dangerous and create less of an impact upon the body. You can still reach some very interesting and old powers in these forgotten temples and it is possible to learn a great deal from them. Once that power passes deep into the Abyss, the consciousness becomes far removed from humanity and therefore becomes dangerous.

There are also natural magical places deep within the consciousness of the planet that the magician can access to work with the land, the weather and ancient sleepers. Accessing these places, which appear to us as deep caves that connect to different mountains, different fault lines etc, via the north threshold can help the magician to build up a series of deep workings that connect vision and ritual. Once the cave has been worked with sufficiently in vision, then the magician begins to open up the north threshold to enable it to lead directly to the cave. Once that is completed, the ritual work done at the north altar will be fed directly into the deep cave; it will be as if you are working ritually at the threshold of the cave itself. This is a method of working that is used when the span of work is going to take months and is a deeply involved piece of magic.

So for example if the magician is working to disperse the inner impact of toxic nuclear dumping in a mountain, the magician would first work in the deep cave that connects to that mountain. The magician would need to keep all the other connected mountains that stem from that cave in equal balance throughout the work, so it is not an easy job. The work would begin in vision deep in the cave and would be a matter of dealing with whatever was made apparent by the inner contacts within that space.

When the visionary aspect of the work is done, then restructuring and reenergising needs to happen. This is done in contacted ritual, where the inner contact is brought back into the room via the north threshold and works with the magician at the altar. The threshold of the north altar becomes a threshold to the cave and the beings, the magician and the ritual patterns flow back and forth over the threshold.

The cave itself can be found either by working in the north parent temple, with the intention of finding the deep 'root' cave of the mountain in question; it usually presents by way of a long twisting deep passageway that goes deep underground and eventually turns into a tunnel that you have to climb or jump down. Another way of finding it is to go in vision to the mountain in question and begin exploring the cave system beneath it. You keep going down and down until you find yourself in the 'root' cave. The key is holding the intention of where you are going; this will help the beings who guard the mountain to see where you want to go, why you want to go there and allow them a chance to decide if they are going to help you find it. If you hold the intention of direction, they will lead you.

Working with Earth/Sand/Stone

Magically working with rock, earth, sand etc is a very interesting experiment and it can be used for a variety of purposes. The basic magical use of rock/earth in the north is for protection/to shield. But it can also be used as storage, to pass on information, to connect with deep faery beings/land beings, and to hold stillness.

Rock can hold vast amounts of power and consciousness with ease and is the most stable of the elements for us as humans. Rocks can hold beings, and can also be home to many different types of beings. Smaller rocks tend to be inhabited by faery beings - not the little giggly Victorian little girls in wee dresses or large breasted scantily clad women with wings- these are fantasy constructs and have no place in magic. Faery beings tend to be very strange looking, often animal like, they can be very big and are certainly not cute by any stretch of the imagination. These beings often inhabit certain rock outcrops and if you are respectful enough, and give them sustenance like food/drink, they will often agree to work with you in vision and to guard you if you need it. In return though, you must keep to anything you agreed to do for them. Pissing off faery beings can make your home really uncomfortable to live in.

Rock can also hold dragon power if it is in an area that the Romans never had access to. They were very good at locking dragon power down, and in the UK you have to go to the Highlands and Islands, or parts of Devon/Cornwall to be able to reach that ancient power that still breathes within the granite. If you have a power or a being that needs putting somewhere, a place where it will agree to go, then rock is a good place to put them. Many different types of beings are happy to live in rock over long periods of time because it is so stable and so connected to the different elements.

Dust and sand can be used for 'sending' power/energy/consciousness if you use it in conjunction with the wind. Charging dust or sand with a power and a purpose, and blowing it out onto the wind of a storm that is blowing in the right direction can be a powerful way to send magic to a place or a person. It can also be used to 'smokescreen' a specific area from the inner vision of other magicians.

Larger rocks can be communed with and their consciousness accessed to ask them to be guardians. They will watch over an area and guard it, and the beings that live within the rock will inform you if there is trouble coming.

The smallest form of rocks, dirt and sand, can be charged with an energetic frequency that spreads from particle to particle. So for example taking a handful of sand and tuning the sand to stillness and silence, and then placing the sand/dirt back where you took it from and mixing it in with the sand/dirt all around it, creates an area of stillness and silence within the land that you can then work with. This method of work needs the magician to have the power and skill of total focus, and the ability to mediate power into substance. That in turn comes from learning about how to work in vision, how to work with ritual intent and how to hold total focus.

Elemental Combinations

Once you have learned in depth how to work with the different elements magically and have worked with the various powers that flow through the directions, you will begin to notice the crossovers and combinations of the powers and elements that work together. Basically, every element is in each direction, and the dominant element modifies or strengthens the other elements to create interesting power combinations.

We see some of these combinations in our myths and legends, such as the sword in the stone, warrior goddesses who operate through springs, swords of fire, and so on. The combined powers of the elemental directions are where magic really comes into its own, and you learn to work the powers like an orchestra conductor. It is truly a form of magical alchemy and the deeper your working knowledge of the elemental powers and their expressions becomes, the deeper you are able to operate as a magician in the inner worlds. The work truly becomes an action of gathering formless powers and mediating them through the elemental directions and into being.

This deep work cannot be done if you do not truly understand the powers, their outer and inner manifestations and how the elements work together. It is not a matter of book learning; rather it is learned from direct experience, inner observation and outer ritual experimentation. This is why the training of the magician cannot be rushed; you cannot speed up understanding and experience no matter what someone promises you.

On a practical level, you can engage this learning experience by working with the different tools in a ritual context in directions that are not their natural home. By working with fire/sword in the north or earth/wand in the west etc, you begin to learn how the tools work with different elemental powers flowing through them. The step on from that would be working in ritual and vision with the different combinations and learning how the power of different directions affects the tools in different ways.

Keep a tight record of all that you do in these combination experiments, so that you can go back over the notes years later to see how the learning curve unfolded for you. It is also interesting once you have done some of that work, to look again at magical texts, or historical and religious texts to see how the snippets of magical power combinations manifest through those traditions. It will give you a deeper understanding of what those writers and artists were trying to quietly convey. This does not really work if you do the reading first and then experiment as you become loaded with pre conceptions and misapprehensions, which in turn can shape and narrow your inner experiences: you come to expect something so the inner connections narrow to fit into that expectation. Your consciousness filters the inner experience and lessens the learning ability. So work first and then read up on the subject matter.

The Four Temples

The four temples are the founding structure of many types of magical, ritual and visionary work. They have many names; the four chapels, the four gates, the four cities, and they appear in Hindu sacred texts along with many other ancient writings. They can appear in many forms depending upon the culture they are flowing through but they all lead back to the same principle; each outer sacred place flows from an inner sacred place which in turn flows from a parent structure that has developed naturally through the inner actions of humanity over millennia. The four temples are the 'parent' structures, inner gateways created by humanity over thousands of years that act as an interface with inner powers, inner contacts etc.

The four elemental temples are thresholds or templates that are the result of generations of priesthoods from many different cultures who reached into the inner worlds. Over thousands of years, different priesthoods have worked with these elemental thresholds and have built their own temples that draw upon these parent structures. Hence, you can access virtually an inner and outer temple in our world by working through these four parent directional temples: they are gateways and contact points for all the inner priesthoods and temples.

The four temples are the formalized expression of the elements Air (east), Fire (south), Water (west) and Earth (north). To us it appears that they all cluster around the central flame out of which all things come; it is a version of the void.

The Temple of Air is associated with learning, formalization, recitation, religions that use a book/text/the word. At a deeper level it is the source of all sacred utterances and patterns; it is the direction of heralding angels, the direction of magical swords, blades and spears. And at its deepest level it is the whirlwind which dismantles and creates.

The Temple of the South is associated with fire, volcanoes, healing, cursing, ceremonies, and bright hot power. It is the direction of the wand or staff and it is connected to electricity, explosions and war. It is the direction of male power and life, of the power of the Sun and of underground fire.

The Temple of the West is associated with the Moon, the fall, the ocean, the sea temples, genetics, and waves of humanity, madness, emotion, sex and death. It is the polarized partner of the Temple of the East; the east being of the intellect and the west being of emotions. The older Christian churches were balanced around this polarization with the altar and priest in the East (knowledge and recitation) and the people in the West (generations and emotions). The waves of humanity flow in and out of the Sea Temple of the West.

The Temple of the North is the temple of the depths of death, the Underworld, the dark Goddess, and the ancestors. It is the temple of time, opening doors to the past and future, thus making it the temple of prophecy. It is the temple of the planet, of gravity, of stone and substance. It is the polar opposite to the Temple of the Sun and in ceremonies the priest will sit or stand in the south and the priestess will stand or sit in the north; the God and Goddess facing each other.

Throughout the life of an esoteric student, they will, in phases, work within the temples in turn. It may not be in a clockwise rotation, but through time they will begin to learn the mysteries of each temple and how they work. Each temple, each element, has a lifetime of learning within it that begins to show us how our universe operates and where we belong within that universe.

The following four visions are old visionary patterns that will take you into the temples so that you can observe and learn. They also tell you a little more about the contacts in those directions and what to expect from them. These are the 'parent' temples from which the elemental powers flow.

These visions can be intense and the best way to work with them until you get used to the pathway, is to record the visions in your own voice and let the recording guide you. Before you record them, read through the text of the vision and identify places where there would need to be a short period of silence to enable you, while deep in vision, to pause, experience and commune with the powers you will be meeting. Put those pauses into the recordings which will enable you to truly strengthen the contact.

Once you have worked with the recordings for a while and have become accustomed to the vision, stop using the recording and work from the memory of how to get there. Once you know how to get there on your own in vision, then you will truly begin to work with the contacts. The vision will change over time; you will find different details, different people and other areas over the thresholds.

The initial vision is not a dogmatic path; it is a map to help you learn how to access these inner places safely. The more you work in these temples, the less detail and 'dressing' you will see – eventually you will simply pass into an inner space that is filled with the power of the element and the consciousness that flows from that element.

But to get to that stage safely, it is important to work slowly through a visionary interface using the imagination, so that your body and consciousness can slowly adjust to the ever deepening powers that flow through these thresholds. The visionary interface known as the four temples is an old one and encompasses millennia of magical work; it is a well trodden path that leads the magician into the inner realms.

The Vision of the Temple of the East

Light a candle and be aware of the direction in which you are seated. Close your eyes and see the candle flame with your inner vision. As you look at the candle flame it grows bigger and bigger until it becomes a column of fire. You step through the fire and find yourself in a large hall full of priests and priestesses who are circling a central flame.

You join them in their meditations and walks, finding yourself walking slowly around the central flame and reflecting upon your life. You begin to notice four gates, one in each direction and each gate has a pair of guardians on either side of the entrances.

A priest or priestess comes to you and places a hand upon your shoulder. They tell you that they will be your sponsor in this place of gathering and they will help you learn about the temples. The contact guides you around the circling of the flame and stops you at the entrance in the East. The angelic guardians look intently at you and you can feel them probing you in great depth. Things that you have done wrong in your life begin to bubble back into your memory and they watch how you react. You look at your memories and you can see where you could have acted differently. And yet, you ponder on the things you have learned through your mistakes and you realize that you gained wisdom and understanding through your actions.

On that realization, the angels step aside, the great doors to the Temple of the East swing open and you enter. You step in a building that has a large archway opposite you and you can see that the archway leads to a deeper part of the building. You find yourself surrounded by hooded or veiled priests and priestesses who wish to greet you. As you look around you can see that they are scribes, working on manuscripts, parchments and blocks of stone. They are preparing books for the library and one of the contacts holds out a book for you to look at. You carefully take the beautifully bound and tooled leather book and look at it. The inscriptions are in a language you do not understand.

The contact shakes his head and shows you how to hold the book to your heart. Upon doing as he asks, you begin to feel a stream of emotion flow through you. You feel many emotions at once and you also begin to feel how those emotions can be turned into power.

The contact takes the book from you and you are led deeper into the temple to a long high ceiling tunnel. The contact stays at the entrance to the tunnel and tells you that he can go no further, that you must continue alone.

You step into the tunnel and a high wind comes from nowhere and tries to blow you back. You lean into the wind and push as hard as you can against it. You inch your way forward through the tunnel until you come to a large elaborate door. Pushing the door open you are faced with a hurricane that tries to blow you back down the tunnel, but somehow you manage to crawl forward to the centre of the small cave. The air is sucked out of your lungs and you feel as if your life might be in danger.

Just as you are about to give up, the wind suddenly stops and you can stand up. You are in a small circular cave that has a large hole in the centre. A tornado twister is raging in the centre, coming down from above and up from below. You tentatively step forward, drawn to the power of the twisting wind.

As you look into the wind you see many eyes looking back at you and you are shocked. Something makes you turn away from the eyes and as you turn your back on the wind, you immediately feel a power building up behind you. Your lungs begin to hurt as though they are straining and you feel something touch you at the back of your neck.

Instinctively you open your mouth: something blows through the back of your neck and the breath comes out through your mouth. The breath turns into words and sounds which in turn transform into shapes.

The shapes travel out of the cave and down the tunnel towards the outside world. The sounds continue to come from your mouth until your body begins to collapse from exhaustion. Instinct tells you to close your mouth and fall forward. Someone picks you up and carries you down the tunnel towards the outer level of the temple.

You are unaware of the contacts around you until you come to the threshold of the temple. When you reach the threshold, open you eyes and look at a large angel that is carrying you carefully. His wings have many eyes and his hair blows in all directions. He breaths gently over you and whispers a word in your ear.

A feeling of great power passes through you and changes you. He carefully puts you down and allows you to step forward over the threshold and back into the main gathering hall: walk straight towards the central flame and step into it.

Bathe in the flame which revives you and when you are ready, step out of the flame and find yourself back in your body, seated before the candle. Sit for a while in silence before carefully opening your eyes.

* * *

The vision of the Temple of the East (air) puts you into direct contact with the stream of consciousness within the inner worlds that deals with the recording of knowledge and the mysteries of air. It has no cultural overlay as it is a template place, and versions of this place will appear in many different cultural, religious and magical streams.

The deeper part of the vision connects the magician to the deeper power of utterance and air as it passes across the abyss and expresses itself down the Tree of Life. In this vision, the magician is on the receiving end of that utterance, and acts as a mediator to bridge that utterance out into the world. It teaches you at a deep level how to mediate the power of air, how to work with the angelic beings that operate around that power and it gives you a solid structure to work with as an interface for that power. Once you have become used to working within this template with the power of air, then you can take the knowledge that you have absorbed, and work with utterance in more depth within the Tree of Life in vision, and work ritually with the power at the altar. The final unfolding of that power would be to work outside, uttering into the wind.

The Vision of the Temple of the South/Temple of the Sun

Light a candle and be aware of the direction in which you are seated. Close your eyes and see the candle flame with your inner vision. As you look at the candle flame it grows bigger and bigger until it becomes a column of fire. You step through the fire and find yourself in a great hall filled with priests and priestesses who are circling a central flame.

You join them in their meditations and walks, finding yourself walking slowly around the central flame and reflecting upon your life. You begin to notice four gates, one in each direction and each gate has a pair of guardians on either side of the entrances.

As you walk around the central flame something draws you to the threshold of the south gate. The angelic guardians look intently at you as they probe you in great depth. The angels look to see your intent, and when they are happy with what they see the angels part and let you pass over the threshold into the Temples of the South.

The sunshine is almost blinding as you step into a bright sunny courtyard with many flowers and plants around. Before you is a gathering of people who seem to be watching something that you cannot see. Edge closer to see what is happening and as you break through the crowd, you will begin to see a life size game of chess in progress.

The chess board is painted out onto the stone flagged floor, and the chess pieces are moved by two helpers. The two players, both elderly men, sit in deep thought as they ponder their next move. One of the old men looks up and sees you in the crowd. He beckons to you to join him. He asks if you would like to take his next move for him. You look at the chess board but you don't recognize many of the pieces. The old men both laugh and one tells you that this is the real chess, that you should try it once, so that you understand it.

They tell you to wander around the pieces until you know by instinct which one to move. Stepping onto the chessboard, you immediately feel the difference; it is like walking on water. Your hands trail over the pieces and with each one you touch, you have a deep knowing that they are not ready to be moved.

One piece seems to begin to glow as you get nearer to it. As your hands touch this piece, a strong feeling comes across you that the piece no longer belongs where it is and it has to be moved. Carefully, you push the piece across the board into a new position. Suddenly, everything changes; the weather, the board and the feeling that is flowing through you.

This action triggers a very strong realization that the piece you moved was connected to someone's life and the action you have taken has changed their life forever. You turn in panic to the old man but he just smiles. The understanding of the power of the Sun Temple begins to reveal itself to you, and you begin to understand how they use power to manipulate for good or bad. The power of this courtyard is the power of conditional change; moulding the world from a particular viewpoint.

Step back from the chessboard with the intention to go deeper into the temple. In the distance you see an old dilapidated rock entrance, almost like a crack, but you can see it has been worked to make it into an entrance. It draws you in. The entrance leads to a long dark tunnel that seems to slope downward and you begin to walk down, deeper and deeper underground. The smell of sulphur begins to rise and it burns your eyes and lips.

The tunnel opens out into a vast rock chamber with volcanic fire in the centre. The fire draws you closer and although you can feel its heat, it does not burn you. A strong impulse overwhelms you to step right up to the fire and lift out your arms as if to embrace its flames. The fire responds and a loud rushing sound builds up around you. Power builds and builds until there is intense pressure upon your ears and the loud sound pierces into your brain.

All at once the pressure drops, the sound stops and many bright spinning wheels of fire dart out from the volcanic flames. They spin around you at high speed, their brightness dazzling you; it is then you notice the wheels have many eyes which look back at you. One of the wheels passes right through you and a feeling of immense power rushes from your feet to your head and back; like a surge of electricity. As it leaves your hands tingle and throb; carefully you place your hands together and the feeling of power subsides.

Someone comes up behind you and places a blanket around you. He scoops you up into his arms and you lay like a child, held by a man with a face of the Sun. His brightness dazzles you and his warmth flows through you, energizing you. He walks back through the temple and carries you to the threshold of the central great hall filled with priests and priestesses. Very carefully he puts you down over the threshold and before he leaves, he places a medallion around your neck. You look down at the medallion and it is the golden image of a man's face that glows with the Sun.

The man withdraws back into the temple and the guardians close ranks to protect the Temple of the Sun. Walk straight back into the central flame and bathe in the flame which revives you and when you are ready, step out to where you were seated before the candle. Sit for a while in silence before carefully opening your eyes.

* * *

Experiencing the Temple of the South puts the magician in direct contact with a specific quality of solar priesthood and will enable the magician to attain a better understanding of the power dynamics that played out in priest-king states. It also introduces the magician to the power of angelic beings that work with fire which in turn will broaden the magician's inner senses of such angelic power when it is time to work through the Tree of Life.

The above vision only touches upon a small section of the power that flows through the south; there are many fire and solar lines of priesthood and power, far too many to list. The key is once you have connected with one strand of priesthood in a direction, it is then much easier to reach for connections with the other strands. If you are working in a specific line of magic that has its roots in an ancient system or culture, the solar line will be very apparent within that line. For example if you are working/learning about the inner aspects of Egyptian magic, then working in vision in the South Temple will enable you to reach for a connection with the priesthood of Ra.

The Vision of the Temple of the West/ the Sea Temple

Light a candle and be aware of the direction in which you are seated. Close your eyes and see the candle flame with your inner vision. As you look at the candle flame it grows bigger and bigger until it becomes a column of fire. Step through the fire and into the great hall of priests and priestesses as they circle the central flame.

Join them in their meditations and walks, finding yourself walking slowly around the central flame and reflecting upon your life. You begin to notice four gates, one in each direction and each gate has a pair of guardians on either side of the entrances.

Circle the flame and stop at the entrance in the West. The angelic guardians look intently at you and you can feel them probing you in great depth. One of them sniffs you and the other one tastes you; they are reading you to make sure they know who you are. When they are satisfied with what they have found they let you pass over the threshold and into the Temple of the West.

A woman greets you as you step over the threshold. She is tall with long red hair and many tattoos adorn her arms and shoulders. She escorts you into the Temple of the West where many priestesses are gathered around something. You look closer and see that they are weaving what looks like a giant web. One of the priestesses offers to show you what she is doing. She hands you a piece of thread and as soon as that thread falls into your hands, you see all of your family. You see your ancestors, your extended family; everyone who is connected to you through blood.

The priestesses gather different threads and tie them together, creating beautiful patterns that in turn create a web that stretches as far as you can see: you realise you are a part of that weave; you can feel yourself within it and yet it is hard to grasp exactly what it is. One of the priestesses watches you with amusement and when you have seen everything of the weave that you need to see, she takes your hand and leads you down a dark tunnel that smells of the sea. You can hear the ocean all around you and water laps around your feet. The two of you emerge through the back of a long cave that opens out onto the beach. The priestess leads you up to the waters edge.

She washes her face in the ocean and motions for you to do likewise. A wonderful feeling of cleansing washes over you with the sea water and as you dry your face and look up, the light of the full moon falls upon your face. You begin to cry and your tears merge with the ocean. The woman places her hands upon your shoulders and you sob as all the pain and suffering that is in your family flows through you and is emptied into the sea.

The woman holds out your hand and gives you a knife. "Give of your blood to the ocean and offer your honour to the Temple of the Sea." With one swift movement, draw a cut across your hand and throw the blood into the sea.

The sea begins to swell and the waves crash over you without pulling you off your feet. The moonlight becomes stronger and the sound of the whales calling lulls you into a deep state of peace. You fall down into the sand and allow the water to wash over you. The moonlight dances over your body, changing and triggering the deepest part of your immune system.

Sleep pulls at you and you vanish into a dark deep peaceful sleep full of dreams that are wild and full of prophecy.

Nothing disturbs you as you drift until a flicker of a flame awakens you. You find yourself back before the candle flame where you first started and when you are ready, you open your eyes.

* * *

Working in the Sea Temple exposes the magician to deep and ancient lines of magic that ebb and flow through our species. This is the place to explore and work if you wish to develop your own innate psychic abilities, learn about the lines of consciousness that runs through your blood line and work in service with the priestesshoods there.

It is a very fluid (ha!) temple and is best worked with in a mutable way: do not try to organise yourself or the powers, or ritualise, formalise or quantify their powers: you will hit a stone wall if you do.

Working in the Sea Temple is instinctive, creative and dreamlike, and when you allow such qualities to guide you, the contact will become strong. It will flow through your outer life and affect everything around you.

The Vision of the Temple of the North/ The Temple of the Dark Goddess

Light a candle and be aware of the direction in which you are seated. Close your eyes and see the candle flame with your inner vision. As you look at the candle flame it grows bigger and bigger until it becomes a column of fire. You step through the fire and find yourself in the great hall of priests and priestesses as they circle the central flame.

You join them in their meditations and walks, finding yourself walking slowly around the central flame and reflecting upon your life. You begin to notice four gates, one in each direction and each gate has a pair of guardians on either side of the entrances.

A priest or priestess comes to you and places a hand upon your shoulder. They tell you that they will be your sponsor and they will help you learn about the temples. They guide you around the circling of the flame and you stop at the entrance in the North. The angelic guardians look intently at you and you can feel them probing you in great depth. One of the angels places a hand upon your chest and you feel the angel asking the organs of your body many questions. When the angel is happy with what he discovers, the two guardians part and allow you to step over the threshold of the Temple of the North.

You find yourself in a dark cave with a pool of water in the centre. Many priestesses and priests are gathered here and are tending to sleeping animals, birds, humans and plants. As you look around the cave, you notice in the shadows the outline of an old lady sitting upon a stone chair. Her hair has grown down into the rock and her arms hold many sleeping animals: she is watching you as you look at her. She nods to acknowledge you and in a strange almost whispered voice tells you to come closer.

The closer you get to her, the more creatures you see hidden in her clothing, in her hair and in her arms. Her long cloak which lies in layers across the floor beyond her has humans curled up asleep in the folds of the dark fabric. Something compels you to touch her feet in reverence and the touch of her skin is cold, like death. She feels your fear and smiles at you with compassion. There is something about her smile that triggers long forgotten memories within you and as those memories begin to surface in your mind, the fear within you falls away.

She tells you to come often and visit her. She will teach you about the land, the rocks and very old magic. In return she asks you for a gift; give her whatever appears in your hands and if it is something you own in life, then you must bury it for her.

One of the priestesses places a hand upon your shoulder and leads you to the back of the cave, behind the goddess, where there is a tunnel cut out of the hard rock. Together you pass down this tunnel which has many strange and beautiful images painted upon the stone. In the distance is a large doorway that is carved out of the stone. Many fabrics hang over the entrance and above the entrance is the face of a demon with her eyes glowing red in the darkness.

You pass through the doors and find yourself in a small dark cave that smells of sulphur. There is very little light and you stumble around until your foot hits something. Kneeling down, you find your hands upon a large smooth stone. The stone breathes beneath your touch and the power of the Goddess in her rawest form passes through you. This is the Goddess in her truest form; that of the Earth, the stone, the planet. You can feel all life in your hands, all existence, and the potential of birth.

Instinctively you place your forehead to the earth and rest your head on the breast of the Mother Earth. She moves under you, and you hear a heartbeat. You merge with her, becoming one with the rock and together you sleep through time as the planet turns around the seasons.

You drift in the stillness and silence, losing all sense of a body, of time, and of your own identity. In your slumber you merge with the rock and feel the passage of the planet through space, the turning of the Earth, the warmth of the Sun and the pull of the Moon. You feel as if you have come home, this is where you belong; you relax deeply into the stillness and drift.

Something, somewhere calls to you. You lift your head and see a doorway. Through the doorway is a candle burning brightly. You lift your hand to your eyes to shield from the unaccustomed light and you edge nearer to have a better look. You see a human sitting before a candle flame. With a shock, you realize that it is you. You go and sit down and merge with yourself, becoming one. When you are ready you open your eyes and blow out the candle.

* * *

Working in vision with the goddess in the cave is a fundamental cornerstone of magic: she is the key contact that anchors magic in the physical world and she also helps you to learn and connect with the land around you. Working with this vision gives your inner self 'roots', it grounds your power while confronting your own fear of death.

Don't fall into the trap of trying to name her: don't be asking is it this goddess? that goddess? She is a deep filter that earth and Underworld goddesses flow from; if you reach for the power behind Cybele, then you would reach this ancient goddess in the cave.

When you have worked for a while with this deep power in vision, you will find that the need for visionary interface falls away and the contact becomes strongest by simply being out in nature. She flows all around you and once you have communed with her in vision, the land itself, all around you, begins to commune with you.

And that holds true for all of the elemental/directional visions. The visions are merely steps, not the end destination. Through working in depth with them, your mind and body changes and the connections between you and the power deepens until the visionary interfaces are no longer needed.

There is no short cut to this level of communion with power; it has to come slowly over time through vision, contact and ritual. But if you persevere, there will come a day when the contacts and powers flow all around you, all the time. Because you have spent so much time working consciously through interfaces (visions/contact), you will instantly recognise the 'signature feel' of a specific power, deity or line of consciousness.

7

Divine Power and its Containers

"With the net, the gift of Anu, held close to his side, he himself raised up IMHULLU the atrocious wind, the tempest, the whirlwind, the hurricane, the wind of four and the wind of seven, the tumid wind worst of all. All seven winds were created and released to savage the guts of Tiamat, they towered behind him. Then the tornado ABUBA his last great ally, the signal for assault, he lifted up. He mounted the storm, his terrible chariot, reins hitched to the side, yoked four in hand the appalling team, sharp poisoned teeth, the Killer, the Pitiless, Trampler, Haste, they knew arts of plunder, skills of murder" - The battle between the Marduk and Tiamat. From the translation of Enuma Elish by N. K. Sandars

Through the Eyes of the Wind

One of the predominant streams of religion and magic in our world today is a stream that comes out of the magical direction of the East and is dominated by recitation, or 'air'. Seeing as we have looked in depth at the elemental expressions and how they flow through magic, I thought it would be interesting to look at the concept of the Sephiroth and the Qliphoth through the magical element of air. The Sephiroth is a Divine Power, and the Qliphoth is the shell that contains the power and acts as a filter between a specific resonance of Divine Power and physical manifestation.

Because the magical direction and power of Air has such a predominance in Western religions and magic, it is a good example to use to look at the power behind some of the deities, the beings and the elemental powers that flow through our lands: the Sephiroth and Qliphoth.

Clues as to the rise in dominance of this 'air' power can be found in ancient texts and with careful study along with in depth inner work, it is possible to track the foundations of certain religions to the release and expression of this Air/East power.

While it is very interesting to go in depth into the ancient creation myths of Sumer, Canaan, Babylon and Egypt, my focus is more upon the inner and magical visionary expressions of this power as opposed to the historical context. However, working from an inner/magical visionary aspect to observe these powers certainly brings the ancient texts into play and they begin to make far more sense. As always, my constant mantra: do and experience first, then go away and read the ancient texts.

Repeatedly the ancient texts tell us of the powers of storm gods, the ones who bring terrible winds, storms that bring chaos, storms that destroy. Often one storm god supplants another, as in the case of Marduk supplanting Enlil, who was an earlier form of the Wind power. This becomes a repeating pattern expressed in a variety of forms across North Africa and the Near East. We find smattered references to storm gods that also are connected with blades and with serpents. Writings can be changed, misinterpreted, supplanted or manipulated to make a point. But the inner experience of these powers is direct: through observing and interacting we can learn the inner source of these stories.

On the surface they appear to be stories that attempt to explain the creation of the world, and man's struggle to understand his environment. But as you magically interact with the environment, you begin to understand a deeper form of the stories and recognise keys that tell you a different story, a story about how to communicate with these primal powers.

The Magical Path to the Elemental Forces

These powers are not human friendly in general, or even human conscious, so the path towards their core is one that can take some time to tread. My treading towards the core container (Qliphoth) of the Wind in the East was not a conscious one, it sort of happened to me despite myself. I do not know if there is a defined ritualised inner path to the threshold and then container of these vast powers, if so, I have never found it. But that does not mean it does not exist. I was sort of funnelled, channelled and occasionally dragged into magical and visionary situations that brought me into various layers of contact with the East Wind power.

Looking back, it is a very clear and defined path that I walked down, a path that brought me deeper and deeper into the mysteries of this power. And yet at the time I had no clue, no idea what was really happening. I thought I was in control, I thought I was making definite magical choices, connecting specifically with inner beings in a way that gave me a broad outlook. In reality, I was being marched like a squirming child down a corridor towards the head-sisters office (I went to convent school). Now, in my 50th year, I stand before that head-sister's door and I can remember exactly what it feels like to be seven years old and in trouble. And boy do I know I'm in trouble.

So it is worth bearing in mind that the magical path and development towards working with these powers can often be haphazard and born out of spontaneous experiences. The more we try and control our progression, the more we end up locking ourselves down. So before we look at the pattern of what a path of development might look like, let's look at the formation of the power itself.

The Primal Force; Divine Power and its Expressions

One of the things I discovered, when I eventually figured out what it was I was working with, is that these primal elemental powers have various expressions that we can perceive and interact with. The source of these primal forces is a Qliphoth or container that holds and gives form to a specific expression of Divine power. The deities and externalised forms flow from this container. The closer you get to the container and its contents (Qliphoth and Sephiroth), the stronger and more powerful the contact is and the more elemental and natural its expression becomes.

The Qliphoth emanate lower octaves of the power of the Sephiroth, and some of those lower octaves can be worked with and formed into a deity. When the deity is formed or adjusted by humans using ritual techniques, it takes on a filter of humanity with all its inherent imbalances. These imbalances can be very unhealthy and probably led to the mystics opinions that the Qliphoths are demons; they are not, but their emanations can be.

Qliphoths

So let's just take some time to look at the Qliphoths, moving away from the overview of Regardie, Crowley et al and going back to the source to look more closely at what is going on from a magical perspective. The word means 'shells' or 'husks' and that is exactly what they are: they are containers that act as filters for Divine/Primal Power. They can manifest as forces of nature, which in turn give us forms that we recognise as deities, demonic beings, Titans etc.

To observe this process we must go back to the Tree of Life and see how Divine Power emanates down the Tree to finally manifest. Once it has crossed the Abyss and begun to take on a patterned structure (This is the point of Daat, which is the mirror of Kether) the power begins to express itself through various qualities, i.e. the Sephiroth, which bring the specific positive and negative qualities of the Divine Power into orbit. The Sephiroth are pure expressions of that Divine Power potential but still has no structure to contain it, nor a filter to manifest itself through that we can, in our imbalanced human form, connect with.

The Qliphoth or shell, surrounds and contains the Divine Power potential, slowing it down in its expression and allowing it to take manifest form. Remember that for power to take form it has to have polar opposites, positive and negative, it has to have tension between the two, so the two expressions of power are constantly of and within one another.

At this stage of the game, the orbit of the negative/positive power inside its shell expresses out through our world as an elemental force that we begin to interact with. That interaction and mediation creates a conversation and through that conversation the container of the power creates a form that we can communicate with and understand better: a primal deity.

Then come the deities that are 'created' through magical action. Through long term ritualised interactions with the primal deity, we create interfaces that are easier for us to commune with, interfaces or substations which have more humanesque qualities; the deities.

The option that Judaism took was to steer as far away from these emanations as possible and work only with the Divine Power itself; hence no filters, no deities etc. That in turn grew the religion into a pattern whereby there is no image of Divine Being, no deities, no filters, only the utterance and its outer expression as a sacred alphabet. This can also cause terrible problems as we have all witnessed through the destructive nature that runs through the Abrahamic religions. But why is such pure communion with Divine Being so potentially easy to corrupt? Because it has no filters and we are imperfect beings. To commune with such pure power, there must be absolute internal discipline, balance and no emotion.

We are inherently imbalanced as spiritual beings by nature of our physical manifestation. Therefore pure Divine Power, unfiltered and unchallenged, hits our imperfections and spins us out of control. The slightest imbalance will be magnified as the power reaches us, because that is what power does. We try to channel and control that power by use of recitation, prayer, self-control, self-denial and the controlling of everything and everyone around us. Those religions call for submission to Divinity, but in doing so, we are driven to balance that by exerting control, usually over others weaker than ourselves.

The Abrahamic religions go to great lengths through laws to teach us how to be balanced, but ultimately the lessons of balance are learned through experience, not through laws. Unfortunately, humanity in general tends to learn best through hardship and bitter experience. Just like cells, we as humans like to take the easiest route possible, expending the least possible energy. The combination of a great deal of power and only budging if we have to does not always make the greatest mix.

The key to the Qliphoth is to work with the singular or least complex forms of deity when at all possible and to have a balance of the Qliphoth without allowing for too much subdivision. Good practical examples of this can be seen in more ancient and early classical religions. For example in ancient Egypt, in the Old Kingdom, you had a smallish group of major deities, linked to elemental powers and the flow of life and death. These deities balanced each other out, and kept the dance of creation and destruction in order under a Divine system called Maat (which was also a goddess who oversaw the system).

Magical priests slowly discovered that you could mirror the act of creation and create a Qliphoth as a filter and container, breathe Divine breath into the Qliphoth (to create a deity) and then split the power of the Qliphoth into subsections. This created 'substations' whereby the inherent qualities of the Divine breath were broken up into fragments to create deities.

Two things happened. The first thing was the ability of these constructed Qliphoth to hold Divine Power was reduced (think of pouring a large jug of water into little egg cups). And the imbalance of humanity passed into the constructed Qliphoth: we cannot play at being Divine, no matter how much we think we can. I suspect this is the source of the destructive and imbalanced Qliphoth so many magicians tap into.

The second thing they found was that by subdividing the deity powers, they were weaker so they could be controlled more. The human need for control overtook the wisdom of power sharing for a greater mediation of power overall. It is harder to lift and control a very large bucket of water to fill something, but it gets the job done. Whereas trying to fill a bath with an eggcup gives you more control and is easier to lift, but far less effective and becomes almost useless.

This is mirrored in the Roman pantheon where they had a god for just about anything and everything. When they figured out that they had subdivided too much and were under threat, they brought in the Magna Mater, the great Mother. As a deity she is one of these expressions of primal power; difficult to control, hard to please and very powerful. Unfortunately for the Romans, although she did save their ass, they did not get the true wisdom of what was happening to them and it all went horribly wrong eventually.

This pattern of behaviour in humanity: connecting with a primal power, building a relationship with it as a deity, learning how to control and subdivide its power, which in turn leads to powerlessness and collapse is seen over and over in the ancient world. We also see aspects of it today in India which still has the mass of subdivided deities in its religions.

Ritual/Magical Orbits

When the Qliphoth are interacted with magically, the dynamic begins to change, become more complex, more powerful and more prone to degeneration. As was discussed above, the basic natural relationship between human and these powers is one of survival, respect and 'listening'. We evolved beyond that and wished to interact more actively, take some control, bargain, manipulate and also to explore.

Staying with the theme of Air, let's look at how this relationship works. As the temple cultures began to evolve, the priesthood skills developed as they worked closely with the angelic mediators/filters. The priesthood learned how to form their own 'Qliphoths' or containers for Divine Power in the form of humanesque or anthropomorphic deities and using the power of the angelic filters, they mediated the power into outer created forms which were then interacted with.

At this stage, the deities were windows for elemental power, with the angelic filters keeping the balance. Usually the deities held both sides of the power, negative and positive and the angelic beings/demonic beings ensured that the power flowed out to the manifest world as it should. The deities would warn the priest/ess hood if a major surge of creation/destruction was on its way – similar to the tribal relationship but more formed, more verbalised. It was at this stage that offerings could be made, covenants struck etc to change the course or expression of the power to suit humanity or the land in general.

This in turn brought about a major shift in the thinking of the priesthood and humanity in general. The temptation to offset danger/destruction and encourage creation/growth was great indeed. Sometimes this bargaining worked, unless the elemental force had a major job to do in which case the filters still gave warning, but the disaster was not averted: the power had to sweep across the land, that was its nature, that was its function.

This failure to control the deity force in full flow brought about the skills in the priest/esshood to develop methods of filtering and subdividing the power in an attempt to fully control it. Powers were split into two deities or more, and priests learned how to change the power expression of a deity by changing its man made Qliphoth, i.e. its 'shell' or inner expression of its outer material form and attributes. They also learned how to manipulate the filters/mediators that worked with the deities by binding the angelic/demonic beings to form and control exactly how they worked.

This can be seen in some of the ancient temple cultures whereby the primal deities have been supplanted by more humanesque deities that take on more 'useful' attributes and where the angelic/demonic filters have been bound into service as guardians, deliverers etc. This is where the guardian spirits/angelic/demonic beings are given names, attributes, functions etc all within a temple service.

The more these powers are contained, bound and controlled, the weaker they become as the filter or window that the powers flow through is subdivided and diluted. Later on in history we see a complete degeneration of the system whereby human made Qliphoth are created with intent but without proper knowledge, leaving an empty container ready for any degenerate and weak being to step into. The human gives it a voice, food and lodging, and the parasitical being enters into a relationship with the human.

What we are seeing with this dynamic is the octave of the creation of the world as it goes through its various levels. The Divine Consciousness is housed in a container that is the world/Malkuth. The container is constantly re-shaping itself as it interacts with a species. The container is further shaped or patterned (emergence of deities) when a specific species (us) engages in direct communion and subsequent relationship. The species then attempts to subvert the process by creating its own containers in an attempt to mimic Divine Consciousness: we try to be God and we believe we can create deities. And that is the stage that we are at now.

One of the ways our forebears tried to step away from this degeneration was to try and build a relationship with Divine Being that was not dependant upon deities, filters and such like (Monotheism). Unfortunately that approach too became quickly degenerate. Maybe the answer is not in the method, but within ourselves?

Pathways and Parasites

The most common way that humans have attempted to create pathways to the Qliphoth and illicit interactions is by the use of magical incantations and spoken rituals (staying with the theme of Air). This can be very good or very bad; much depends upon the spiritual integrity and purity of the intent of the ritual and the ability of the magician/ priest to form and manipulate power. If a religious recitation or magical incantation/ritual is focussed upon supremacy of a single deity/being (not Divinity) at the expense of all others, and re affirms its power expression in our world, then invariably it is going to bring disharmony, imbalance and destruction. We see this played out with elements of the Abrahamic religions. If the filter is heavily littered with controlling dogmas, particularly ones that evoke strong emotions, then there is a very good chance that a parasitical being has moved in and is operating the filter/religion through the priesthood.

These parasitical beings are beings within their own right, have certain mediation powers, are often conditional and can be elemental, demonic, deity or even thought forms: they can and often are any type of being. The main feature is that they step into a man made container for their own agenda, which is usually a search for a source of energy. The real/natural Qliphoths are immune to such infestation; they are a much higher octave and whatever they emanate, for good or bad, is the power of Divine Consciousness.

A man-made Qliphoth however is as flawed as its creator and even if one of these containers survives for thousands of years, it will still carry the inherent imbalance of humanity. That imbalance not only attracts parasitical beings, it also enables them to move into the container and operate it indefinitely.

The way to avoid ending up with a parasitic Qliphothic creation is to ensure that you are working with a deity that has firm roots in the elemental powers, has established positive and negative and is a 'known' image or identity that can be traced back for a long time. There are many of these parasitic Qliphoths around these days, particularly in the magical community in the form of 'edgy' deities such as 'Babalon', 'Lilith' and 'Baphomet'. These 'deities' were constructed out of psychopomp, bad reading of history/theology and no inner connections. There is nothing 'evil' or 'bad' about these containers, they are merely man-made structures that can only mediate limited flows of powers with the parasitic beings that have stepped into them to do 'business'.

These more modern containers developed as a result of human focus, repeated use and a cooperative parasite willing to help construct a new source of dinner for itself. But these are not the highly crafted man made Qliphoth that emerged in the ancient world which are in a magical class all of their own. To spot them, look at a culture and look at its early deities. Then look at the subsequent generations of deities and their subdivision of power: that is usually the junction point for created Qliphoth. It will also indicate a time of instability with the nation and its rulers. Whether this is a direct result of the subdivision, or if the instability spurred a priesthood to attempt to acquire more control, who knows? Either way, what we do know from history is that when humanity attempts to interfere with the Qliphoth or tries to create its own Qliphoth, it all goes horribly wrong.

Now it becomes clearer why Qliphoth were and are considered demonic or 'bad'. The shells themselves are not bad; it is a natural dynamic that once power begins to takes form and become exteriorised/moulded, the potential for corruption is vastly increased. Add humanity in to the mix and the potential for corruption is overwhelming. That is the nature of power manifest and externalised: if it is 'born' out into the manifest world, it also has to 'die' and withdraw from the manifest world.

Essentially, the Qliphoth protect the pure balance of Divinity from the imbalance of humanity and visa versa: they keep Divinity and Humanity apart in a constant magnetic orbit.

Deities/Qliphoth and Lots of Wind

The wind is only balanced when it is expressing itself naturally, and from a magical perspective is in balance and context with all the other deities that mirror the various forces of nature. Once it is expressed through a deity that demands singular worship above all other deities and that demand is adhered to, then the balance spins out of control. Its negative powers are expressed through religion that becomes 'supreme'. This in turn manifests the East Wind power as dogmatic control, aggression and destruction.

We see the steps of this in many of the ancient religions in the form of initial contact with a listening human, to a covenant often sealed with sacrifice/blood, and then the subsequent spin out in humanity in the form of dogmatic word/utterance of laws, prophecies and eventually war.

Often the original elemental/nature deity is supplanted artificially by a priesthood (subdivision or man-made Qliphoth) with a more aggressive one, which leads me to suspect that this is the point where another more parasitical being steps into the frame with a promise; you do this for me and I will do that for you. So it goes from a relationship of understanding and mutual respect, to one of control and supplication.

We can see this repeated in various Near Eastern religions in their early phases such as the Sumerian pantheon. Enlil, the storm God was balanced out by Ninlil the wind goddess (who is probably the root of the later demon Lilith). Their relationship was one of balance and counter balance and their union created other deities. An interesting aside that I came across magically, is a repeating pattern of connection with the power of the wind, and the descent into and emergence from the Underworld.

Eventually Enlil, a storm god that visited the storms of nature upon the land became supplanted by Marduk, a god 'who controlled the winds', a storm deity, the son of the sun, who became the patron god of Babylon. His titles included ones like 'Lord of Lords', and 'Supreme Lord'; he was a warrior, a leader, a magician and most definitely a force to be reckoned with.

Similarly in ancient Egypt, first we have the older god Shu, the wind in balance with his sister Tefnut, the moisture. Later, she faded into the background, and by the New Kingdom another god of wind was rising in prominence. Amun supplanted Shu as the one to talk to about the wind/weather, a god who became more prominent than the others and was considered the saviour of Egypt in the battle to expel the Hyksos.

Like Marduk, he had far more skills to his bow that Shu did, just as Marduk had a wider range of power access that Enlil did. For example in a stele, Amun is declared as: "Lord of truth, father of the gods, maker of men, creator of all animals, Lord of things that are, creator of the staff of life."

He was appealed to in storms: "The tempest moves aside for the sailor who remembers the name of Amun. The storm becomes a sweet breeze for he who invokes His name." So the relationship between man and the deity has moved from one of warning/call to action, to one of supplication and control.

Ba'al Hadad/Adad storm-god in the North Semitic/Babylonian pantheon again is a close echo of Marduk and a possible root of the Semitic god Yahweh who some scholars now connect with the attributes of a storm god.

These storm deities that have wider attributes (bulls, sun, war, kingship, land requisition etc), deities that supplanted earlier wind/storm gods, often demand total obedience and exclusivity. From this we see the development both religiously and magically of systems that mediate a wide variety of powers that often bring war and conflict. Lots of smiting, battles, covenants and promises of power!

Working with the Qliphoths

In essence, working with the Qliphoth is working with the formed power that flows through a deity/filter and approaching it with the understanding of the shell, its make up, its function and its abilities, as opposed to mindless worship or a wish to control through magic. The Qliphoths are the powers behind the deities; the Qliphoths are the bridges that connect raw Divine Power in a first filtered form (Sephiroth) and deity expressions/physical manifestations. The Qliphoths are the gates to the Divine Sparks which in turn are steps towards the Divine Universal Power.

With the birth of psychology and the break up of the Victorian moralistic sexually repressed society, magic was looked at, theorised over and experimented with as a vehicle to break away from the tight bonds of an uptight society. Throw into the mix the exotic fashion of anything Eastern or foreign is mystical and 'deep', and you have a cooking pot that is potentially disastrous for magic.

I am not saying that the exploration of the darker side of humanity was not fruitful, these pioneers forged new paths in how we think and how we approach power. But at the same time, in their glee of being 'dark' and 'edgy', they created a system of working within Kabbalah, i.e. The Tree of Death and the Demonic Qliphoth that while it was 'exciting', it diverted attention away from the real depth of these powers. It's like putting a McBurger and a sirloin steak on a table: people have run to partake of the McBurger and completely missed the sirloin.

The first and most important thing to do if you want to work with a Qliphoth is to look closely at its deity expression attributes from an outer point of view. If it is a deity that has been worshipped/been around for a very long time and has not had other deities grafted to it (Amun-Ra is a graft example), then there is a chance that this container of power is not overly diluted. The further back you go in history, the clearer the expressions get.

The second thing to look for is to ensure that it has two sides to its attributes: a good creative side and a darker destructive side. This tells us that the access route to the threshold of the Sephiroth contained within the Qliphoth is one that is healthy: it accesses the positive and negative powers of the Sephiroth, it is balanced. The Qliphoth is also a complete expression i.e. creative and destructive, so it too is balanced and this will express through a deity that has both opposing powers within it.

If the darker or lighter side has been fragmented into a separate deity, so long as they work together as a team to keep each other in check, then the power is still contained and balanced. If however only one side of the equation is expressed, there is a huge potential for imbalanced power and the Qliphoth expression is probably a human construct. This can happen if the Qliphoth has been magically manipulated to suppress one end of its power spectrum. The result would be deities emanating from this Qliphoth that are one sided, unbalanced and therefore destructive even if their emanations are creative... it will mediate a power of destructive overgrowth.

The third thing to look at is whether the natural primal forces have been filtered down into controlled use for human consumption. For example, let's go back to the Primal Wind (a Qliphoth). If we look at it through the deity Enlil, we will see that he is primarily a storm god, referred to as the god of the north wind. He is presented as male, as a potential destructive wind that also brings rain and winter. His partner is Ninlil, the goddess of the southern wind that brings warmth and growth. They are both connected to agriculture with Enlil providing the tools and Ninlil providing the seeds.

Although the Qliphoth presents two deities, their power is still focussed, is complementary and they work in orbit around one another: two opposing forces that are of one another and yet work in harmony as a combined force. They reflect the duality of the Divine Power within the Sephiroth. That is a very important point: the primal force of the wind manifests as two deities, Enlil and Ninlil; but they are still only one Qliphoth. If those deities are subdivided again and again, it will still be only one Qliphoth that is expressed through a multitude of deities: the power of the Qliphoth is merely diluted over and over until its ability to express the power of the Sephiroth is too dispersed to work with.

Where this all went terribly wrong in human terms, is the supplanting of these two opposing primal forces through further human tinkering. Enlil and Ninlil as primal deities were too powerful to manipulate and eventually the priesthood understood how to fragment and tinker with the Qliphoth to subdivide or supplant the deity. Enlil was overtaken by Marduk, storm god and warrior with many different attributes (Sun, bull, kingship etc) who immediately demanded that only he be worshipped and worked with as the god. You start to see the process spinning out of balance and breaking down.

Once you have found a balanced deity to work with, and its attendant beings, then it is time to begin to work in vision and ritual to step through the deity to the Qliphoth beyond. Don't forget, a window or threshold is a two way street. To do this safely, it is advisable to first work in depth with the deity so that you really understand the power dynamics that it mediates. This would be done first by working in ritual with the deity, then in vision within the confines of the human realm, and then finally in vision in the inner temple of the deity.

Now you can start to see why it is so important that the deity you work with is in fact a true deity and not a human created shell: for this passage deep into the power of the Qliphoth it is important to be able to pass through the inner patterns of the inner temple of that deity. Such interactions with an inner structure will help you form a safe path to the seat of power and will also provide you with the necessary beings to help facilitate such a connection for you. You cannot truly just wander up to a Qliphoth, a real container of Divine Power, because not only would you not find it, but you would not be able to communicate with it without filters.

The inner temple of the deity provides filters, paths and safeguards. In return you are of course expected to mediate that Qliphoth power into the inner temple and then out into the world. There are no free rides; you work for your supper.

Approaching the Qliphoth Through the Inner Temple

When working in the inner temple of the deity, there are a few different ways that you can approach the Qliphoth behind the deity. The first route would be through the knowledge of those who have served the deity in the past, plus the knowledge of those who shaped the deity and first interacted with it. That collective knowledge is expressed as a library. Working in the library in vision, you would hold the intent to connect with the powers behind the deity and with that intention you would build or clear a path through the library in increments.

Once you are at the end of that path, you would probably find yourself stood before what appears to be nothing, but feels like it is filled with everything. That is the threshold of the Qliphoth. Beyond that is the spark of Divine Being taking form (Sephiroth) which for us as humans is unapproachable. The threshold of the Qliphoth is held in place by two opposing archangelic forces whose job it is to stop you crossing that threshold. Rather than force the issue and get catapulted out, it is a good idea simply to come to this place with the intention of going no further and simply being there, on that threshold, in a state of silence and peace.

This simplicity achieves a couple of things. It allows your body to normalise to the level of power there and it allows the threshold to normalise towards you. You could spend the rest of your life stood at that threshold in vision and it would be time well spent. Why? Because you will be in orbit around the Qliphoth and therefore in orbit along with the deities: you take your place in the pattern of orbits that start with Divine Consciousness and ends with humanity.

By being at peace and in stillness, there is no agenda, no 'container' of wants or needs to fill. This allows you to eventually become a mediator of the power emanating from the Qliphoth, allowing it to flow through you into the inner temple. In turn, as you leave the inner temple, you can take that power out with you and let it flow through you out into the world. Once this has been done, you become an open door for this power flow.

There is no shut off valve and no moving on; it will constantly ebb and flow through you. Being in the orbit of the Qliphoth will cause the Sephiroth within you to resonate with the Sephiroth within the Qliphoth. We are all octaves of the same power, we are all expressions of Divinity within substance, and we are all, in reality, Qliphoths that contain a spark of Divine Being.

8

The Dead, the Living and the Living Dead

When old friends come to visit

In *Magical Knowledge II*, I talk about the death process from a visionary/ inner perspective and the chapter talks about how to work in vision with someone who has just died. In this chapter I will talk about the dead from an outer perspective, in terms of how they interact with the world of the living through presence, haunting etc and how we can live magically with the dead living alongside us.

Not every person who dies goes straight onto the path of deep death to emerge into another life. Some stay around the living, some sink deep into the land to wait, and some, dependant upon culture, stay within the land to act as an interface with the living. As magicians, the dead who choose to stay in our world in various ways can be contacts that we can work with, or they can be a part of our service as we care for them and give them shelter. It is not a popular branch of magic in the Western Tradition; many societies and religions of today tend to view the dead with suspicion and fear. This is a sad degeneration and something which has generally fuelled a fear of death which in turn becomes deeply embedded in our psyche.

There is a fragment of wisdom in such fear; clinging to the dead is unhealthy for all concerned and forcing the dead to stay and work is definitely an unhealthy way to work magic. But like everything else in life, the truth of a situation is often quite complex with many variables and no one rule will work for everything.

Working with the Dead

Working with the dead who present themselves to the magician is a major part of the ancient path of magic and is an opportunity for great learning, needful service and establishing bonds with the past.

This much ignored area of magic gives us a deeper understanding of the nature of life and death, and helps us to work with a sense of our own death, so that we die in a more fulfilled and balanced way. Death work in all its forms, be it vision, ritual, working with the dead and tending the dead has always been a major part of the mysteries from very ancient times and it is something that really needs bringing back into the fore of our consciousness.

Working with the newly dead is a form of magical service: you make sure everyone goes where they need to go and that no other beings, particularly parasitical beings, are hitching a ride with the dead person. Often the newly dead who make a presence known just need acknowledgment that they are still existing, help getting any unsettled business out of the way and then pointing them in the right direction on their journey.

Work with the longer term dead and the ancestral dead tends to be more about making connections with the land spirits, bridging information back and forth between the living and the dead; it is a chance to learn lost skills and work with the long term dead who are still in the land by assisting them in service they are performing (i.e. Sleepers). These contacts also tend to warn you of impending major danger, intense dangerous weather/earthquakes etc that are coming so that you can act accordingly. They can also act as advisors and guardians but treat the advice as you would advice from any human: just because someone is dead does not mean they are all knowing. They will see things you do not, but you will also have perspectives that they do not. You must use your common sense when working with this type of consciousness.

The Dead

When we die, if we have a strong spiritual/religious pattern that has a clear path through death, we tend to follow that path without question until we get to a phase where we no longer need that pattern: the veils part when the time is right and we are able to move forward through death.

So for example if you are an active Christian Baptist, after the initial shock of death the consciousness begins to emerge again and the spirit of the person will 'see' and 'be' within a Christian setting. That will continue until the person begins the process of letting go. First they let go of loved ones, belongings etc, then comes the shedding of the personal identity. Once that identity begins to break up, there is no need for the religious structure to give the spirit a vocabulary, and the spirit begins to engage directly with the powers and beings that work within death.

From there the spirit will make a choice to either rest, merge with Divinity, go into a new life, or if they are magical/spiritual adepts they will stay in the inner worlds as an inner contact/guide/teacher (which is not the same as the dead hanging around the land). Some dead stay in a phase of death which enables them to stay within the land and keep communion with the living; the Catholics call this purgatory (God's waiting room), a place within death where life can still be reached.

The spirit of the person can flow back and forth between the living and the dead, and they are usually still connected to the body they left behind. So if the body is buried as opposed to cremated, they will still have a connection to that body. When a spirit is in this phase it can be communed with in inner vision through the death vision or they can be communicated with in the physical place where they have chosen to 'hang out'. This is also the situation where most haunting stems from.

Then there are those who are still very much locked within their bodies and bones. Sometimes this locking in is a result of ritual or binding and sometimes it is the result of the culture of the person who died. This can be perceived from a magical perspective by working with the burial or bones in ritual, in vision and with the outer manifestations that express themselves in areas close to the body in question.

After working with burials for a long period of time I have discovered that a strange dynamic sometimes happens with long term burial whereby the spirit of the dead person begins to interact and then merge with the consciousness of a land spirit so that they commune together with the living as a hive being. The symbiotic relationship of two very different types of consciousness, for example an ancient sleeper and a faery being, enables the spirit of the dead and the spirit of the land to communicate with the surrounding humans in order to pass on information regarding upcoming events that would threaten the tribe.

Although these close knit tribal communities living closely with the 'sleepers' has long since gone from many areas around the world, these contacts can still be worked with, which is something we will discuss later in the chapter.

The Newly Dead

People who have recently died often get an urge to tell their loved ones that they still exist. The success of this largely depends upon the culture, beliefs and ritual actions of the living family members, and it also depends upon the natural capacity of the living to pick up upon the 'cues' attempted by the dead.

Some cultures do not encourage communion with the dead, and a small amount of cultures will actively 'shut down' any chance for the dead to make a connection. This manifests itself as the covering or removing of all pictures of the dead person, the refusal to utter the name of the dead, and the keeping up of prayers or religious rituals to move the dead on quickly whether they like it or not.

Another barrier for the newly dead to communicate is the aggressive refusal to acknowledge life after death, so any 'cues' the dead person may achieve will be ignored or explained away. In some aspects, this can be healthy in that it encourages the dead person to let go of the living and recognise that their connections in life are now over; the living loved ones can no longer exist for them. This spurs the newly dead to reach quickly into death and to let go of everything: it moves them on.

In my younger days, I felt that this was always the best way forward for the dead, but over the years various experiences have taught me that the process is not so easy, cut and dried: people need to go through the very different stages of death in their own time and some who stay behind often have very good reasons for doing so.

The attempt to make contact often (but not always) comes within a few days of death and takes on many different forms depending on the state of mind and ability of both the dead and the living. It is worth bearing in mind that previous cultures that had a good relationship with death would often have stories that outlined and taught people how a spirit can communicate and what cues to look for. The learning of these stories in life also embedded the strongest methods of communication deep into the consciousness of the person, so it would be knowledge available upon death: it would be second nature. Modern thinking and dogmatic religions have wiped a lot of this from our consciousness as individuals and as a community, so really we have stepped backwards in a sense.

It takes time for a dead person to work out how to affect something in the physical world and for some it takes longer than others. Some never figure it out at all and some do not feel the need for it, so not every dead person is going to try and communicate. The usual first attempts involve something that has a high energy source, something that can be energetically triggered easily. In a house that would normally manifest as the dead person working out how to affect electricity and the objects that electricity flows through.

For us in our house that has manifested as all the light-bulbs blowing, the TV going nuts, the computers going haywire etc. When my mother (who was a natural but undeveloped psychic) died she visited our house within a few days. She managed to blow every light-bulb in the house and made the TV commit suicide.

She also visited my daughter's house and my nieces' house where she managed to blow the light-bulbs again and finally backed off her light-bulb Armageddon when I told her that she was welcome for as long as she wanted to stay and that we were proud of her. She hung around and worked with me until the funeral, after which she moved deeper into death.

My cousin died a few months later and again we had to replace all the light-bulbs. But this time he hung around a lot longer and would emit bursts of armpit smell in the hallway. He had been slowly dying from a terrible illness and had suffered a great deal of pain: he was frightened, traumatised and needed shelter. It took me a little while to figure out that it was still him once he moved away from blowing light-bulbs and began his armpit routine. The shift was probably brought about by him relaxing (and therefore not blowing things) and allowing the trauma of his last year of life to surface. The smell he emitted (along with the scent of alcohol) was a bitter smell of illness: he was still in that place and was struggling to get away from it.

I let him hang out with us and he even came on a day trip with us, which was a bit weird, but slowly the hallway smell changed from very sick man smell to his own natural presence. He was an interesting man, also psychic but again undeveloped and his ability never had any outlet in life. It was a pleasure to be able to share this space with him and give him shelter.

Smell is another 'cue' used by the newly dead. A sense of smell for us is a very strong sense, deeply embedded in our brains and is one of the last senses to go as we die. It also seems to be a sense that is the easiest to trigger in the living by the dead: it is a quick and easy way to say, 'I'm still here'. When my maternal grandmother died, I was at my mother's house and half way down the stairs, my grandmother's very individual perfume would waft all around me. Again this stopped after the funeral and she went on her way. She was just saying goodbye to her family.

And that is what most visits from newly dead are about: they want to let you know they still exist and to say goodbye. A simple acknowledgement of them both verbally out loud and in your mind is often all that is needed. Sometimes they do wish to stay around for a little longer and sometimes, when you are a magician, it is for magical reasons.

The dead are not all knowing, but they do see things that we do not, just as we see and do things they cannot. When you are a magician/priest/ess working at any reasonable power level, you will be exposed now and then to dangers and these dangers are often picked up on by the dead. They will try to warn you, to protect you or to even deal with things for you. This has happened to me a few times where I asked a newly dead friend or family member if they wanted me to escort them through death and the answer was a resounding no. They wanted to work alongside me or protect my back as I worked for a period of time. Once the threat was over, they would withdraw.

Once when this happened to me, and the dead person withdrew, I assumed they had moved deeper into death. In my linear time, it had been a few years since the death, and they had initially worked with me for a couple of months (a dear friend and magician) and then they had vanished. Ten years later they suddenly appeared again and worked intensively to protect me during a difficult situation. I worked in vision to communicate with them and asked why they had not moved on. The answer I got back was that they were about to move on, they just had a few jobs to do first.

After a rather confusing conversation, I realised that they were not in 'time', i.e. there was no time for them and they were 'seeing' situations that they felt they needed to be a part of and once that was done they would walk into death and back into life.

The incident in my life that happened just after their death, and then a further incident ten years later were all happening at the same time for them. They were not hanging around for years and years, rather they were popping into the flow of life as they saw need to and that flow was at different stages of time in the physical world. I found that fascinating: they were not aware of the lapses of time in my life. It changed dramatically how I perceived the dead and how it worked for them and it also cleared up for me so many unanswered questions I had struggled with.

For example a priestess friend of mine who died appeared to me shortly after death and then a few months later. I worked with them in the death vision for two weeks and slowly walked them through death and beyond. But years later they appeared to me again at a time of need and I could not understand how they had come back after going into death so deeply. What had happened is that when they died, they saw 'lights' go on in friends who really needed help, and they attended to those lights as any priestess would. Once that was done, they walked deeper into death to sleep, ready to be reborn.

To us, those 'lights' going on in friends/fellow priests in need would have been scattered over decades but to the dead it is happening all at once. Our living concept of time is only really applicable to substance, but not to spirit or consciousness.

So if you get a visit from the newly dead and your microwave blows up or your lights all die, just tell them well done, you are proud of them and they are welcome to be with you until they are ready to move on, which is often not long at all. It is worth remembering however, that most houses of magicians have magical tools knocking about the house, deities in rooms etc: many of these things will block out the dead. It is compassionate to have one area or room of your home that does not have anything magical in it that will block out the dead, so that they have a place of sanctuary.

Fear of the dead is unwarranted and has no place in a magician's world: it is the product of Hollywood, cheap novels and dogmatic decaying religions.

Living with the Dead

Our current culture dictates that the dead are unclean zombies that want to eat our faces off, and should be avoided at all costs. People raised with a fear of the dead and an ignorance of the dying process have that fear embedded within them from a early age and it can be a terrible struggle to overcome it. But really, the dead that hang around are more frightened and confused than you are a lot of the time and as a magician, it is important to confront and then dissolve irrational fears that stop you from doing your work.

The dead seek out those who can potentially hear or see or feel them, and they seek out people whom they hope will not ignore them. Often they want something specific, sometimes they want to be around you for a short while, particularly if they are family members, or they may want to guard you, or stay a while to bathe in the energy around magic. The reasons for staying around are as numerous as humans are, and some reasons are good and some are bad.

If you choose to let a ghost stay in your house, keep a constant awareness of them when you do magic so that you do not accidently catapult them out of the house. Do not give them offerings, as this would encourage parasites to come along for the ride: this in turn can result in the dead person having to try and fight off a parasite that wants to use their spirit to interface through and demand more 'food'. A normal dead person will not ask for things of substance; they will want songs, they will want you to remember them and acknowledge them. If they start asking for food, drink, tobacco etc, then you have either a composite being (dead person and land spirit) or something masquerading as the dead in hope for an energetic meal: know what it is you are letting live in your home.

The resident dead will come and go, sometimes vanishing for months before returning. Just let them do their thing and you do yours: you really begin to forget they are there until they try to catch your attention for a reason. As a working magician, they can be very helpful in letting you know what is coming, if there is danger around you etc. This is kind of a modern version of the ancient sleepers (see below towards the end of the chapter). You learn to work together by close observation of the cues that the ghost puts out and finding ways to communicate productively.

I use a mix of Tarot, listening, dreaming, smells, sounds and occasionally having a phone thrown at me (a desperate attempt by a ghost to say, talk to me!!) but you must learn not to become reliant upon the dead in your work and they have to learn to detach from their reliance upon the living. They will vanish when they are ready, and when that happens, you know you have done a good job for them.

Longer Term Haunting

This can get very interesting though complicated depending upon when in time the ghost was a live person. If you are actively seeking a connection with the dead around you, and wish to work with them magically, then there are a few things you need to take into consideration. One important point to take on board is that the cultural, magical and religious understanding of the long term dead can often be very different from our modern day perspective. This can cause a great deal of misunderstanding on both sides, so it is wise to tread carefully and take nothing for granted.

Usually, long term dead (hundreds of years or more in our terms) tend to be tied to a particular place and they are there for a good reason. If you wish to work with them magically, then you need to understand what it is they are doing so that you do not inadvertently damage their work or block it in any way. To understand what they are doing you need to investigate the social, religious and cultural aspects of their time. In the UK, if someone was from a few hundred years ago then chances are their reason for staying is family or property based: they will be guarding or trying to interact with a family most likely no longer there.

The culture in England over the last 1000 years or so has been broadly Christian based and that has to be taken into account. It will be a rare ghost indeed that is willing to work with a magician if they are from that time span. But if you push further back, then you are moving into the realm of Saxon, Roman, Celtic or Pictish society on this land: they are more likely to be still around because they are guarding something, usually a sacred burial or a special place, etc. Again you have to take this into account and realise that they will be more or less limited to working in that area and in a limited capacity.

Working with the Ancient Dead/Sleepers

Once you stretch back (in the UK) to earlier pre Celtic tribal societies, things change dramatically in terms of magical intercommunications. In Britain, you are probably talking Bronze Age, Neolithic and back in time from there. In countries like the US you would only have to reach back a few hundred years: it really depends upon the land, its history and the people who have lived there.

These older societies worked very differently from ours and this is as true for their dead. Ancient burials have sleepers, watchers, guardians, etc all of whom played an important role in the upkeep and general well-being of the tribe. Some tribes would have special burials around them or in key places and these would act as 'sleepers'. Sometimes the bones of certain dead would be carried around as a working member of the tribe, to be consulted and to bring along their protection etc.

As magicians we can work with these burials if they are willing to work with us and the methods of approach, communion and interaction with these ancient burials are very different from working with more recent dead. With the ancient dead, you have to automatically presume that there is a land spirit interwoven with the consciousness of the ancestor. While it may not always be the case, treating the burial as if it was makes life a lot easier and the communion gets going a lot quicker.

When the consciousness of a person has been deep in the land for a long time it begins to connect with and interact with the spirits of the land around the burial and over time the two merge, at least from our perspective. When you go and talk to an ancient burial, if they agree to talk back to you, you are potentially accessing wisdom and information from both the dead and the consciousness of the land spirits in that area.

There are a multitude of faery tales, myths and legends of princesses, warriors, queens, kings and even armies sleeping in the depths of a hill and who will come alive when they are needed most by the nation/tribe. These tales can be found all over the world and careful study of these old myths and stories can tell the magician a great deal about the power of the land around them. This is an echo of the old wisdom of these burials and as magicians we can tap into them, if they wish to commune with us. Sometimes they just tell you to piss off. Sometimes the bones/burials are there but the spirits/souls have gone. Let's look in more depth at techniques for working with these phenomena.

Working with Burials or Bones

There are a few different ways of working with the long dead who are still around and the first thing to think about is why are they still around? Sometimes they are still there because they are angry and are waiting for revenge; something to be aware of and a good reason to tread carefully. Sometimes they are ritually trapped because of some crime they committed in their own culture, or they were cast out for reasons that we may not understand. Not every ancient burial is one that is good to connect with, so caution is always a by word.

Often an ancient (to us) soul is still within the land because of a sense of service to the people living on the land; these are often referred to as sleepers in some cultures. As we know from history, populations shift and change as do cultures, but the burials will often not really differentiate so long as certain key elements of communion are activated.

These keys depend largely upon the cultural framework of the burial and the spiritual belief system that they operated through in life. The longer they sleep in the land, the more the surface cultural interface dissolves until what is left is a broader understanding held by the sleeper. So certain elements of communion with the living will be loosened, but the underlying sense of service will still be there.

For example, a sleeper in the British Isles will be concerned with the health of the land and people, protecting against invasion, and warning about coming weather or natural disasters. Roots of this can be found in the story of Bran in British mythology, and also in the later stories that are scattered throughout the European landscape; stories of warriors sleeping in hills and mountains.

In India and Pakistan there are Sufi saints from the 14th/15th/ 16th century who's tombs are a focal point for both Muslims and Hindus who are searching for spiritual peace, a sense of balance and harmony within the mixed population. The saints remain within the tombs and act as an interface to guide those who visit them, connecting to the pilgrims through their dreams, prayers and experiences.

We also see this within Catholicism around the world where saints are visited for help with specific things, usually illness and disaster. What is interesting with this presentation is that often the bones of the saints are the focal point rather than a burial itself. Often the bones were not of particular people, (there was a lot of dodgy relic business going on in times past) but the tuned focus of people's prayers over hundreds of years has created a spiritual interface or threshold that beings can operate quite well through.

The burial of Tin Hinan, a matriarch of the Berber tribe, was a focal point for the tribes and people would go to sleep upon her burial mound and interact with her through their dreams. Similarly the sleeper in the high Altai region of Mongolia known popularly as the Ice Maiden was considered the keeper of the tribes upon that land and today the tribal authorities are in conflict with the Russian Government over the return of her body.

These ancient burials are very important for us magically as they are a direct magical link to the past, the present and the future of the land/tribes, and from a magical perspective it is important to continue that generational interact with them in a way that is acceptable to the sleeper.

The first rule of thumb is to throw out any 'New Age' ideas of connecting through leaving crystals, plastic ribbons, and other such mindless trash. Each regional burial will have generated stories among the people that guide a person on the right approach to a burial. I spoke in *Magical Knowledge II* about visionary working methods for working with sleepers, so here I will concentrate upon the outer methods.

If you are not certain about how to approach a burial, there are some overall methods that are very simple and that have universal language. One is the giving of gifts that every tribe around the world would appreciate, and the second is the connection through blood and utterance. All of these things would be recognised in a tribal society and still would be today.

Honey is a universal commodity that breaks down barriers. It is full of magical energy, it harms nothing if it is left out in the environment, and it has always been valuable. Giving good quality honey as a gift to the ancestors by placing it upon the land (not in its jar! Smear it on a rock or pour on top of the burial) gives energy to the spirits, feeds the land and the creatures, and always scores points with ancestors. It breaks the ice and is a 'good manners' gift to help open lines of communication. The only burial this would not be given to is one that is still very much within a religious or cultural framework, such as the Sufi burials, where an imam will overlook the interactions, tell you what gifts to give and where to pray etc.

When trying to connect to a tribal burial, once the honey is given, a song or poem is the next step. Again, in times past where the skill of music was only displayed on rare visits by wandering musicians or poets, then such an offering has high status. By singing or reciting, you catch the deeper attention of the burial guardians and also show that you have respect for the person buried there: you are taking the time to connect with them. The next step would be to prick your finger and leave a drop of your blood upon the burial: you are giving of yourself and all your ancestors before you to honour and connect with the bloodlines.

Magically this is all gentle and yet can be very powerful in the building of a relationship with a sleeper. Once the blood is dropped, sit quietly upon the mound and just be still. How do you feel? Have your emotions shifted? The emotions are a good gauge of power interactions with spirits. If you feel still, or happy, or comfortable, then you have settled the guardians and will be able to build a connection with the sleeper. If you feel anxious, afraid or uncomfortable, chances are the guardians want you to leave, for whatever reason. If this happens, then leave the burial alone.

The next step is to find the way that the sleeper interacts. It can be through dreams, through vision work or through outer keys. If it is through direct vision, you will have an almost overwhelming desire to go in vision and talk to the sleeper, seeing yourself go either down into the mound, or to stand in vision upon the land and connect with them.

If they work through dreams, you will be prompted to pick up a bit of earth, or a small stone and take it home to put under your pillow or leave in your bedroom. Or you could do what I do, which is to lay down upon the mound and promptly fall asleep. Dream work with sleepers can be difficult if you are from very different cultures: the visual and emotive keys given by sleepers can be heavily misunderstood if you do not know the mythological patterns of that culture.

Sleepers or ancient burials work within their own framework from the time when they lived, so they may talk in dreams through creatures, birds, patterns, or land presentations. If that happens and you do not understand what is being shown to you, then try to research further into the myths and stories of that culture.

If the sleeper is powerful, then they may try to connect with you through external cues or keys. This could be the appearance of a specific bird, insect, animal etc at times of importance. Again you would need to be able to read those keys in context of the tribal stories of that person.

A lot of this work is experimental: we have lost so much knowledge around this phenomenon and we can only regain ground through trial and error. It will also be dependant upon your own culture, and the ability to be open minded and yet able to differentiate between fantasy and reality in terms of visions and dreams. The older the sleeper or ancient ancestor, the more mythological their presentations will be in terms of keys and visual language.

One thing that can be a major help is to ensure that you try as much as possible to see the world from their perspective, what they would find acceptable and not acceptable, and not what you feel they would want, or what you feel you need or wish to do. Approaching some of these powerful sleepers with an egocentric 'heal me, teach me, empower me' attitude can result in a hard slap or you may simply be ignored.

Another very important thing to think about is where is the burial in relation to you? If you travel some distance to connect with a sleeper, you have to be aware that they are often only operative within a small radius of the burial. So for example dream work will often only happen if you sleep on or near the burial. Saying that, there are exceptions where certain burials have long reaching action across the land; you really have to figure that one out as you work. Some burials are meant to be only occasionally visited, and these tend to be ones that offer help, advice, and guidance, like the Sufi saints for example. That is where the concept of pilgrimage came from.

If you live close to the burial that you wish to work with then a much deeper relationship can be built over time but that again comes with its downsides. Unless you keep within clear magical boundaries of what you are willing and able to offer the burial, you can end up with the spirit of the sleeper trying to take up your whole life by demanding attention, work and also dictating what other kinds of magic you can do. You need to think long and hard about what level of communion and service you are willing to offer.

Working with Bones

At the time of writing this, Vodou and similar paths are the height of fashion in the current magical community. These paths work directly with bones in a variety of ways and some are very successful, but a lot of thought needs to go into what affect that is having upon the spirit connected to the bones and how that relates in a wider sense to the land and spirits around you.

There is a brisk market at the moment for buying bones from around the world and working with them. When you do this, you have no idea of the culture or the spiritual interface of the person who was connected to the bones, what type of person they were or what their intentions are. This can open a huge bag of worms as it is using a magical interface without knowing all the parameters, so you have no idea what you are potentially working with.

In this current age of the internet, cultural appropriation is big business and people have been told if their intentions are ok, then all will be ok. That is not necessarily true and magical dynamics do not work that way. Bones can just be bones, with no spirit connection within them, or they can be still heavily connected to the person who once was constructed with those bones. There is no way to tell until you have the bones in your home and by then it can be too late! So many magicians these days see the old custom of working with a skull, for example, but they often do not think about how this process came about in times past. In today's world you can buy one, which circumvents the whole magical filtering process and places you in a very different line of power which can be very unhealthy at worst, and useless at best.

There are some easy magical ways to deal with these problems and the first way to avoid such a mess is care in how the bones come to you. If you are at a magical phase, regardless of what magical path you are walking, where it is time to work with the long term dead, then bones will come to you. They will either be given as an unexpected gift, or you will find them.

Instead of getting excited and acting like a kid with a new toy, it is better to tread cautiously and find out as much about the bones as you can from a magical perspective. This can be done through using a divination vocabulary like Tarot or what works best for you and asking questions such as; is there still a spirit connected to the bone? Are they ritually bound there? Who is this person (a male/female, elder, magician, priest/ess, mother, father etc)? What do they need from you? And are they willing to work with me?

If bones and particularly skulls come to you through magical ways/gifts/finds, then chances are there is a job to be done, for them and for you. This is how inner magical filters work. You will come to a stage in your magical life where it is important to learn a specific magical skill, and the tools to enable you to learn that something will turn up on your doorstep. Bear in mind if this happens, then the 'learning' will come about through you being prompted to do a job: that is how this form of learning works.

Just being willing to work with what crosses your path and being open minded facilitates the inner flows of power to work with and through you. So what comes to you is meant to be with you. The other dynamic to be aware of is sometimes they wish to be with you for a limited length of time in which case you have to be willing and able to let go of them when the time comes.

This is harder if you have spent hundreds of dollars and taken ages to find the skull only to have to bury it or pass it on when the time comes. It is also about taking magic out of the toy box mentality, and working as a real magician whereby you are able to accept and let go of power as it flows in and out of your life.

Working with the bones and skulls can take a variety of forms and how it works will depend upon the power/spirit within the bones, what they need and what you are trying to achieve. Sometimes they become prophetic tools or voices of warning or teachers that operates through your visions and dreams. Sometimes they are more outward tools in that they simply live alongside you and slowly drip feed you information, or they guard a space or open gates within your work/living space. The key, as with all powerful magical things, is to be open minded, clear and watchful: be able to spot the method of interaction that the bones are using be they dreams, visions, nudging your emotions, being present at workings, etc. If you are observant both of your space and your mind, the work method will become apparent to you and that method will be far more powerful than any method dictated by a current magical trend.

The exception to that rule is where you are still living within the culture that the bones came from and you are still operating within a traditional path of magic that the spirit of the bones recognises. That is becoming a rarity these days, but still does exist. In such a case, the spiritual path and cultural context that you and the bones are in will dictate how best to work with the bones. But for most of us, that gem is no longer available.

I have the skull of an ancestor that lived and died in the land upon which I now live. She is of a similar genetic line to me and is approximately Bronze Age. She came to me unexpectedly, worked with me for a while and taught me a great deal about the powers in the land around me. Then one day she impressed upon me the need for her to go to sleep for a while, so she was placed into a casket and hidden away to sleep. It is very important to respect the wishes of the spirits within the bones and be sensitive to their wishes.

It is the sad reality of modern life that we have to relearn so much and that is best done through direct experience and paying attention! Often the ancient bones that have spirit connections also have land beings intertwined within the contact, so it is also wise to bear that in mind as a possibility. In such cases, it is often possible to directly connect with the land being beyond the bones and the bones act almost like an introduction. This will become apparent if the signs and connections that flow from the bones affect you out on the land away from the bones. It is not that the spirit of the ancestor that is following you around; it is more likely that the land being that connected to you through the bones has a sufficient connection with you to be able to commune with you at will.

If this is the case, you will be able to slowly ascertain the 'territory' of the land being by being aware of when the contact fades as you travel further away from your home. The beings I connected to through the skull fade off within a couple of miles from my home, so the land spirit that is entwined within the skull/spirit of the dead is very specific to the land area around the village where I live. The skull came from farm land around the village and the contact is very much about that specific land/beings/power contained within the land; it connects with me through external signs and dreams.

Your Own Death

One of the major cornerstones of the Mysteries is learning how to die properly from a magical perspective. This is approached in the magician's training by learning how to work in death in vision, how to go through the full death visionary process in life and to learn how to interact with the beings that work within death in all its stages.

The death vision itself that Western Mystery magicians work with is an ancient template of vision that allows us, through controlled use of the imagination in structured vision, to interact with the powers, energies and beings within death and to learn the various stages that the spirit goes through. Working with this first as a learning process and then later in service by working in vision with the newly dead prepares us at a deep level for an important step that all souls must go through.

The difference between the death of a magician/priestess and the death of a non magician or mystic is that the magician/priestess knows at the deepest level of their being what to do, how to react and how to interact with death, so that the transition is conscious and deliberate in terms of the spirit. Different cultures and mysteries around the world all have their own version of the inner passage of death and some are very similar.

The visionary interface that we use is for the living, to form boundaries and images that allow our deepest selves to interact, communicate and learn. The images themselves are not that important in that they are merely a vocabulary for our brains to decipher what is happening at an energetic level. With long term practice, the interface images fall away and we move into a deeper energetic pattern where we learn how to be with such power in gnosis.

Alongside the visionary training, there are outer details that also need understanding, practicalities that stand alongside the inner wisdom of death and together they ensure that the magician, upon death, moves forward unfettered, calmly and with deliberate intent towards their next step of existence. The inner visionary process is dealt with in *Magical Knowledge II* so here we will look at the outer practicalities.

Death can be slow and expected or sudden and out of the blue. If the death is sudden, then there are certain preparations that cannot be done, but there are many others that can be. It is not something to cast your mind to in older age, but is a process that stretches through your life and is an integral part of your magical life.

Letting Go

The first hurdle that needs to be overcome in life is the ability to let go. It is a major sticking point for many in both life and death as our culture these days encourages people to cling to everything and everyone.

The letting go covers everything in our lives and it is important that when something comes to an end, be it a job, a relationship, a house, an object, a person, that we are able to understand that everything is temporary and has a limited life span. Being able to accept change and loss, to be able to pick one's self up and move on is a major maturing within magic and life itself. People cling to lovers that wish to move on, people hoard or cling to objects they have no use for, they morn the death of someone to the point of destruction and refuse to accept change. This creates stagnation in power and in life.

There are simple ways to teach oneself how to move on, let go and grow. The first is letting go of objects of desire if they serve no real purpose with you but will for someone else. Practice giving things you really love to other people so that it can give them pleasure; practice sharing, if you have two coats where you only need one, then give the other one away to someone who has none. It's not rocket science and it is not a new concept, but it is a part of the outer mysteries.

If you lose the dream job of your life, then instead of descending into depression, look forward to the future; when the door slams shut, climb out of the window. If someone you love dies, mourn them, and then move on. They no longer exist in that form and although you may have wonderful memories, you must not pull them back with your pain. Let go of the grudges; in general, do not hang on to things. This can all sound very 'New Age' but it is not, it is a true dynamic of power flowing in and out of your life. I have been through it all, I have lost the jobs, the home, the loved ones, all belongings, everything I cared about, on more than one occasion. But I survived and grew from it because I was willing to let go and move on, to find new horizons, forge new paths, and to find interesting new things to clog my home up with after everything was taken from me.

On an inner level, this ability to let go develops an interesting dynamic and allows you to be more fluid with power: it stops you from stagnating and ending up in emotional paralysis, which is something that hits many people when they die.

Knowing What Death Looks Like

It is also important to know about the processes of death so that they do not catch you unawares. Dying can be a peaceful process or it can get messy, it depends how you are dying. I have been at many bedsides and roadsides as people have died, and the process can vary enormously. If you have a large family or if you work in a hospital or emergency services then you will probably see this for yourself. You can volunteer to sit with people who are alone and dying, a very magical service that will teach you a lot about the human spirit and the processes that we go through.

Be also aware that dying can be painful, it can be accompanied by the vomiting of blood, voiding of bowels/bladder, choking, fits, or it can be a slow drifting in and out, or a passage in sleep or coma. Either way, from a magician's perspective, the most important thing is stillness and connecting with that.

This takes us back to the very first thing that should be learned as a student magician which is the skill of stillness and going into the void. If that has been learned and worked with over a long period of time, it becomes a deep second nature that follows intention. It can also kick in automatically in times of stress, danger and death. The more it is worked with, the deeper the experience and the skill level becomes until it is like breathing. I have been close to the death threshold physically a couple of times, as have many of us, and the deep stillness that the void brings allows us to view the prospect of death without emotion, but simply as a process. As the beings appear, we recognise them, understand them and we do not panic.

There is no one point in life that is your death time, rather there are a few points of contact scattered throughout your life: one will take you, whereas the others may take you close, giving you a preview of what is to come. Some people will have many of these points in their life and some may only have one or two. Either way, the more you work with death, the more you recognise it and are able to deal with it.

A major skill to learn in life that has major bearing on the death of a magician is discipline of controlling wants and needs. For a non magician, this is of little relevance in death terms, but for a magician it is a major tool. As the spirit begins to go through the death process, the spirit still reflects the image, feelings and wants/needs of the body it has just left. Part of the death process is the wiping out of memory, to cull the connections, loves, needs and passions of life which in turn allows us to walk forward unfettered. This process is triggered by an urge which can become unbearable. Whatever the culture/beliefs a person comes from, that urge will present itself; the visionary interface we use in life to recognise that urge can differ from culture to culture, but the dynamic is the same.

In the Western mysteries visionary interface it presents as a terrible thirst that grips the spirit as they travel across the desert towards the river of death and the mountains beyond (plain of Lethe). This is an ancient pattern used within the mysteries (the descent of Aeneis into the Underworld, for example) and although it is looked upon by non magicians as allegory, it is not. It is the magical story interface that the spirit remembers so that it knows what to do: the ancients hid the patterns of the mysteries in the myths and stories of the time.

As the spirit reaches the river, a non initiate will drink to fill their thirst. An initiate of the mysteries will simply wash their face to rid themselves of the identity connected to the face, but they will not drink; this enables them to retain their memories and their magical training will ensure that they are not affected by their memories. This is achieved by strong internal discipline within life, to not give the body everything it desires but only what it needs and only when it needs it. This internal discipline stays deeply embedded within the psyche so that upon death, the spirit has the instinct of control.

By working in the death vision in life, and learning to control and temper basic instincts, the initiate learns to be able to act from a deep place of understanding rather than be driven by impulse. This in turn allows the initiate to make informed and controlled decisions about whether to continue in the cycle of life and death, or to step out of that cycle and work as an inner contact, or if their work in life is finished, to move deeper into the inner worlds beyond life. It is a major step in our deeper development to not be driven purely by instinct, but to engage the powers of existence consciously: the step into true gnosis.

What to Do Magically When You Know You Are Dying

However the act of dying occurs, so long as you are conscious there are things you can engage, if it is possible, to smooth the passing both for yourself and for those whom you are connected to. If you die while unconscious, then it is the deeper training of the spirit that takes over, hence the active learning of death in life to a point where it is second nature.

If you know you are at the point of going, it is really important to withdraw emotionally and intellectually from everyone and everything around you. Don't worry about any loved ones who are around you, nor worry about their emotional or physical wellbeing. It is important to focus upon your own process; the rest of the world around you will take care of itself. This is a simple but very important dynamic: the first stage of letting go of everything and everyone, both for you and for everyone else.

As an initiate, be still, forget your memories and emotions, even if you are in pain: there is a threshold within the stillness that steps you to one side of the pain so that it is still there but it begins to wash through you rather than grip you. Focus on the stillness and the sense of stepping forward into the void: keep a sense of moving forward, going into something. This enables the spirit upon the point of death to immediately step forward into the journey: it is an energy dynamic of birth and death rather than an actual 'movement': the vibration/ energy of our pattern shifts and to us it is perceived as a 'movement', such as the 'turning' into life and 'forward action' of death.

The other important thing to remember upon the point of death is to drop the fear. There is no need for a fear of death: this is why again it is important as a magician to work in death while in life. You get to see for yourself how it works and what it is like, first from a visionary interface in meditation, and later by spontaneous experiences. The spontaneous experiences of death begin to happen after you have worked through the visionary interface of death for a while. You cannot predict when it will happen, only that it will.

It arrives in a couple of forms; one is in very vivid and powerful dreams, usually at key times and the other is through being taken to the threshold of death by illness or accident. It can come to you in both forms or in one of them. When it presents in dream form, you will know what it is. I will not describe it as it is important that you experience it for yourself and that you experience the confirmation of it from outer sources. You will dream various forms of death in very vivid ways as is needful for you, and it will be very clear it is a magical contacted dream. Shortly afterwards, you will come across a text or a painting that exactly describes what you experienced. It is really important that it is a genuine experience and not coloured by my or anyone else's description before hand.

I had two very vivid dreams, years apart, which showed me various stages of death. Each time, within weeks, I was given a book or a picture, randomly and out of the blue that was exactly what I had seen and was an ancient description of the death mysteries from two very different cultures. I mentioned this to a magical elder I respect who explained that the same had happened to him and to his teacher in turn. It is just something that happens within the mysteries as you work through the layers.

The physical taking to the threshold can also happen where you nearly die but do not; in that process you are given a glimpse (no, not light/tunnels, aunty May or Jesus, or landscapes of happy virgins etc) as death literally gets in your face. You may see the pattern of death, or the being that bridges you from life to death (in the Western Mysteries it is an angel of death).

Either or both of these experiences will teach you a lot at a very deep level about what the process will be like for you, so when you do stand on the threshold of death when it is your time, you will step forward in full knowledge and confidence. It is a major transition yes, it can be a difficult transition yes, but it is also an amazing, powerful and magical transition; it is not an end, you as a being do survive and are aware of that survival, just in a non physical form. That understanding does away with the fear of the unknown which is very important, so that you transition intelligently.

The other fear that grips people is unfinished business or the protection of dependants/children. If the business that is unfinished is about the physical world, then you have to let go of that business, as there is basically nothing you can do about it. If it is emotive, basically the same rule applies but with some leeway. There is a period of time after death and before burial where you can say goodbye, visit etc. You can also use this time to intervene magically where needed if you see one of your very close family/friends is in a dangerous magical situation and is out of their depth. It may not correlate to the time between your death and burial in terrestrial terms, as there is no time within death. But it is a time when if you are focussed, you can look at the wider patterns that were connected to your life, and see if there is an absolute need for intervention for someone. You will perceive it at that time, just after death, but in material world terms, it could be happening at any time.

I have had help in certain situations which has come from family members just after their death. But usually the help came at that material time, before their burial, when I was in sore need of magical guidance and help with a very difficult situation.

The more you look into death from an esoteric point of view the more you begin to see how and why it is important that you go into death with gnosis, in wisdom and stillness, so that you can actively engage with the process and be consciously aware of what is happening to you.

Over the years, I have had enough startling experiences while working with the dead to begin to understand the process (and to have extinguished doubts, though questioning yourself is always important) and realise how powerful, complex and beautiful the whole process is. The only real way to learn about death is to work from within it magically, and hopefully the fragments of information in this chapter will help others to find their own magical 'feet' within death and to take the work further.

9

Weaving Power into Form

Chatting with the Three Fates

When you start to really dig deep into the power of magic and use the combination of inner and outer patterns of ritual/vision to instigate a magical action, something very interesting starts to happen. You become aware of the waves/frequencies of power that are constantly flowing in and out of our physical world.

In the visionary pattern of the Tree of Life, or what I call the desert landscape, we observe in vision formless power flowing to us from Divinity across the Abyss, passing through a complex pattern at the point of Daat (i.e. Metatron Cube/ a focussed collection of thresholds/filters which in magic is perceived as angelic beings) that begins to form the power into manifestation which completes itself as it passes over the threshold of Malkuth. From there, the completed power expresses itself out in the world as high frequency/vibrating energy which eventually becomes physical matter. This can be perceived as waves of power/frequency/vibration that underpin physical expression, but also underpin or at least affect none physical expression, like thought, emotion, magic etc. We can observe this energy wave if we stand in vision on the threshold of Malkuth and once our minds have been introduced to the phenomena in vision it becomes much easier to then perceive it in the world around us.

When we are conducting magic at a level of frequency that corresponds to one of these 'waves' of expressed power, we tap into that wave briefly which gives our magic a massive boost (ever done a small magical working and had a massive effect way beyond what you expected?). In turn, our conscious magical action that is in harmony with the wave adds to the stream of energy, giving it a small boost for a second, or alters it slightly.

I have found these waves to be far more powerful than we can currently comprehend and they seem to be the power source or tide for changes in consciousness, in weather, or in civilisations, physical matter etc. Some of these expressions, in human terms, are vast and we tap into them briefly but will probably never understand the eventual externalised results. As the wave slows its frequency or organises itself into a discernable outer pattern, it manifests into something, be it huge changes in consciousness, or physical expression such as a natural event.

As magicians we can and often do, without realising, tap into and interact with these power streams as we conduct a magical act. But to tap into them consciously for a specific purpose we need to understand what frequency of power that wave is, how that eventually manifests and how it will affect what we do. That is currently beyond my understanding and dragged up a whole bunch of questions of cause/effect and responsibility.

I think this is where the concept of a conditional action with an unconditional intent comes into play. So for example, we can be aware of a particular wave of power building up and consciously engage it, i.e. through ritual/vision/weaving, but without a specific intent other than to be a link in the chain. This particular action changes the human action from magician (manipulation) to priest (serving).

It can be used intentionally for conditional purpose, i.e. riding the wave, if it is a power that is compatible with what you are trying to achieve, by tapping into the power of the wave to drive what magical pattern you are working with. For myself, I would be wary of such action until I have a better understanding of what I was actually interacting with. It may be akin to plugging into nuclear power to light a light-bulb, with all its inherent problems.

To intentionally work with this source of power needs a certain level of plasticity in the thinking and working method of the magician: the ability or skill to work in more abstract ways than the usual ritual and vision work undertaken by the average magician. This plasticity comes from being able to think outside the box, while also having a solid foundation of magical understanding and experience to draw upon. You start with what you know works and develop your experimentation from that foundation.

If the dogmatic patterns of a magical path are strictly adhered to, then such abstract work is virtually impossible and if the magician has very little in the way of foundation training and experience, then the consciousness of the magician is often too feral to be able to sustain the complex and disciplined actions needed to interact with these powers. Studying for example of the mysteries of Kabbalah can potentially prepare a magician to work with these power patterns if the study is not weighed down with religious overlay or hazy New Age 'feel good' thinking.

Working in ritual and vision using a method whereby that the patterns of power themselves, their elemental expressions and physical manifestations are acknowledged without any need to dress them in belief structures allows the magician to first learn to recognise power at work and then to engage actively with that power.

It will not be within the capabilities of every magician to be able to pick up on these power fluctuations but for those who can, it can be a very interesting experience to move beyond the simple recognition that there is something powerful going on, and to consciously, actively engage with it. I developed my own method of working with these waves of power, using vision and outer action; I experimented with engaging the power and painting, writing, and 'blind' ritual energy weaving. By that I mean standing in vision and 'seeing' these waves of power, and using hand movements to 'weave' the power into a substance be it rock, paper, fabric etc.

This active engagement of power/energy can also be used in group ritual; tapping into the waves in walking vision, bringing them through into the ritual action and working with it as a group. It can be used to affect necessary change within the land if it is woven/mediated into the land beneath you as you work. The conscious use of the power to affect change using focussed thought and action certainly does seem to engage this power and tune it to specific effect.

What are the long term consequences of engaging with this power? I have no idea as I have not been experimenting in this way long enough to know. This is where keeping tight diaries and records is important so that every step discovered is recorded and any long term effects can be referred back to the original working method. That way, we learn what to do, what not to do, and what needs adjusting in terms of working practice, intent, preparation etc.

Around the same time that I discovered this phenomena (maybe I have re invented a wheel that everyone except me knows about?) I began to come across pictures, writings, temples etc of ancient weaving goddesses and finally understood the deeper mechanics behind their power. I had always known that the idea of a weaver goddess as a basket maker/goddess of weavers was utter nonsense, but the more abstract idea of a weaver of the universe was interesting but I had no direct experience of such action. But they started showing up everywhere all of a sudden as if to say... did you get that?

It then occurred to me to experiment in many different ways with this wave of power, not only as a power source, but learning from it about how things can be built, dismantled and maintained.

Using the Weaving Skills in Magical Defence

Once you have understood the dynamics of power/wave/pattern forming, you then begin to realise that all magic is essentially constructed by manipulating the power into patterns and then launching them.

It does not matter what deity, what spirit, what sigil or what utterance was used in a magical attack, for it to take form and work it must have power and that power must have form. The patterns are formed by the type of magic used and the beings involved in that work. The intent fires it and off it goes.

Usually to dismantle a magical attack/curse/binding that has been formed and sent, you would work within the tradition of the sender, or work with the same type of beings to take the attack apart. If the attack is simple, then that is all that is required. But if the attack is dangerous, large and fuelled by a group of people then you need to reach underneath the surface presentation and take the living structure apart or reform it. Reforming and reusing it is an interesting way to work through these problems as it tends to kill more birds with one stone, so to speak.

The technique itself is simple, but relies heavily upon the magician's mental focus, discipline and visionary skills. The first step is to identify what elemental fuel has been used in the attack, i.e. fire, water, earth, air etc. So for example if it was fire, the first step is to light a flame. The magician focuses upon the flame, seeing it in their inner vision simultaneously with their physical eyes.

Once that focus is there, the magician begins to 'tune in' to the feel of the attack and who or what has been attacked. Looking at the flame, the magician uses her imagination to 'see' the attack in a 3 D pattern form within the flame. That image is built up until the magician becomes aware of the beings involved within the attack: once the inner pattern is exposed within the element, it becomes easier to discern what beings are also structured as part of the attack.

The magician then asks the beings to 'pull the pattern out tight', like stretching chewing gum, which breaks up the outer presentation of the attack without losing the power or contacts that drive it. The magician imagines the power pattern changing from a 3 D pattern in the flame to a pulled out 2 D image, similar to a loom weave or long threads pulled tight. This is the beginning of working with the wave pattern of power and learning how to manipulate and change it, albeit in a very small way.

Once that pattern has been pulled tight, essentially wiping clean the structure of the attack, then it is time to use the raw materials to build a proactive protection. Instead of the magician using the power to weave a protection around herself, which has so many inherent problems which go with such an action, the magician begins to weave a protection that filters the magic at source. Working with the beings involved with the pattern, the magician asks the beings to reform the pattern with her, to create a filter that will be placed over the attacker, like a badly knitted sweater. The filter is to be designed to filter out all reference, contact, connection, image etc of the magician so that the attacker can no longer see them or connect with them energetically:

the person who is on the receiving end of the attack simply energetically vanishes.

The directions given to the working beings needs to be specific: create this filter to filter out anything to do with victim: when the attacker has this filter placed over them, they can no longer perceive the victim magically or through readings/perceptions, they cannot energetically connect in any way; the victim simply vanishes from the reach of the attacker.

All of this is uttered into the flame with the stretched out pattern and the magician observes as the beings reform the pattern into a new shape. Once the new shape is ready and the magician is sure that the instructions are correct, then it is time to engage the filter. This is done by once more focusing upon the pattern in the flame and focusing upon the intent to send it back to whoever sent the magic in the first place. The magician tells the flame, the pattern and the beings that the filter will be placed on and all around the original attacker so that they can no longer see, perceive or connect in any way with the magician. Upon that declaration, the flame is blown out and the power sent off to go and do its job.

This is done a couple of times a day until the curse/bindings/attack begins to dismantle and fade off. Usually it just takes a few days and then it is up to the magician to keep an eye out to ensure all stays calm. If the attacker is clever or has a deep understanding of magic, they will eventually discover the filter and find a way to take it off. So it is important to keep awareness and also learn to adapt and change protection methods.

This method, besides being very effective, also teaches the magician about how power can be woven and how to 'see' weaves of power which in turn prepares the magician for deeper engagement with the waves of power that flow from Malkuth.

Pattern Recycling

Once the magician grasps the enormity of the revelation that everything around them is fuelled and shaped by energy which has its own wave pattern and that pattern can be restructured using magic, then the magical doors really start to open. It is this fundamental understanding of the patterning of power that underpins all magic; it does not matter what system, what path, what religion, what philosophy is used, the pattern of power is where the magic flows from. All the rest of the dressing is just that. That is not to say that systems and paths are not important; they are, very much so. The paths and systems of magic enable the budding magician to grasp concepts, learn skills, have boundaries, and facilitate the first interactions of power through the filters of the path.

But over time the magician begins to understand that the path is only a lens or a filter for the magician to look through; the actual magic is power/energy and how that power/energy is interacted with. At this stage, it is a good training for the magician to work on perceptions of this power and its natural waves in everyday life. Everything has a natural pattern within it that can be not only perceived, but interacted with and manipulated. I began to experiment, using a flame; I would look into the flame and focus upon seeing the pattern of the door/wall/cupboard/plant behind the flame. I looked through the flame to see the world around me in a different way.

Using this method takes time and practice: the brain needs to learn how to interpret the data it receives so that your mind can build up an understanding of what it is you are observing. My first observation was that natural things like a tree, a plant, a rock etc had a certain quality of pattern that was very harmonious. The patterns themselves were very different, but they all had a defined quality of 'neatness' about them. Furniture, man-made objects etc however were a very different matter. Their patterns were diffuse in some cases and complex or over structured in others. Some patterns were clumsy and dense, others haphazard. I was fascinated. It took me a little while to realise what it was I was seeing in this exercise.

The man-made objects were created from different substances that each had their own pattern. The different patterns had been squished together and it kind of worked with some objects and was rather chaotic with others. I then began to experiment with trying to alter the inner patterns of various man-made objects and something began to feel very familiar: I realised I was looking at a deeper method of enlivening sacred objects and creating magic with substance.

When a statue or image is enlivened or a deity is mediated into substance, obviously (duh!) the pattern of the substance itself changes to accommodate such a power shift. I know I knew that intellectually, but I had never actually 'seen' it or experienced it so directly. By experimenting and observing, I was able to discern the changes to the energetic power and frequency of the substance when it was worked upon magically. By recognising that change and recognising what it changed into, I was able to identify the 'signature' of a specific energy change. So for example, enlivening a statue with the power of a deity, I experienced a very specific change in the energy pattern of the structure of the substance. It harmonised the slightly chaotic pattern of a man-made statue and changed it into a beautiful harmonic pattern that shone with power. Cool!

I have found the use of the flame to be the easiest elemental form to use for such power observations, with water coming in a close second. It did take me a while to build up the capacity to be able to perceive and work with these waves and patterns, and I achieved it simply through perseverance and practice. Essentially you are training your imagination to work in a specific way, to imagine seeing patterns in a flame while also looking at the flame with your eyes open. It does take time to get used to that. But once the brain gets the idea of what you are trying to achieve, it all begins to click into place. Don't worry about the age old magical dilemma of 'is it just my own imagination or I am seeing the real thing'. With practice you will begin to notice the difference. The reality will take you by surprise. It always does!

Working with Weaver Goddesses

Once you have worked with basic power weaving, then is the time to look in depth at the weaver goddesses and it will give you a much deeper understanding of their power. In our modern day interpretations of these goddesses, the historians look upon these goddesses as weavers of cloth and thus connect them to early agriculture etc. Nothing could be further from the magical truth of their power.

When you work with these deities, the first thing you realise is that these goddesses are not only ancient and very powerful, but they also preside over war, death and fate. The deities Neith (Egypt), Frigg (Scandinavia), and the Greek Moirai; the three Fates, are examples among many Northern Hemisphere goddesses who preside over fate, weaving existence and the outcomes of war, or are presented as warrior goddesses.

Using the knowledge and experience gained in working magically with power weaving, as magicians we can work closely with these deities to repair damage done to fate patterns by the use of magical attacks. To try and interfere with a fate path or war outcome for our own agenda would be folly, but we can work unconditionally with these goddesses to try and understand the long term impact of fate upon a nation, a people or a bloodline. We can also assist or partake of the action by working as assistants with these powers, following their path of action and agenda, not our own. It is very important when you are working with such ancient and powerful goddesses to understand when it is safe to actively partake of fate weaving and when it is not.

If a human has constructed magic that is interfering with a fate path, then it is acceptable for a human to intervene and alter that interference with the help of these goddesses. If we appeal to these powers for help, say in times of severe conflict, and they agree to help, then assisting them by working in vision or ritual with them is also ok. But it is important that you follow their lead, their action and their agenda, not your own; *they know what they are doing, you do not.*

If however you are simply curious or you have a specific agenda and try to work through these deities to weave the power yourself, you are most likely to get a backlash of an unpleasant nature. It would be akin to a child going into an industrial carpet weaving factory and placing their hands in the mechanised looms.

However, if you are wishing to work upon yourself, or wish to work on something small particularly if it is a problem caused by magic, then working with and through them is fine, but ask first. Tell the deities what you are trying to achieve, ask them if it is wise to do what you are trying to do and if all is ok, then work through them or have them work through you to achieve what it is you are trying to do.

So for example if you wished to work upon someone or something whose pattern had been damaged by magical actions then you would start the action from the exteriorisation. Firstly you would tune the altar you are working with to the weaver goddess that you work with, and ask her if she would be willing to work with you on the task. Some people commune with the deities using vision, others use a conversation interface through Tarot readings. Experiment with what works best for you.

Magical Weaving

You will need a candle, an altar or table as a focus to work upon, and a bowl to burn paper in. You will also need paper and a pen.

The first action of exteriorisation would be to draw out a pattern that represents the person: you are attempting to exteriorise the inner pattern of the person or object to be worked upon. It is very much an act of creationand intuition: follow your instincts and learn to work freely without need to strict steps and rules. The name of the person or place would be around and within the pattern and the drawing out of the pattern would include the areas of damage. Do not express these areas of damage intellectually; rather allow your imagination to guide you. This way, the deity can begin to work through you from the very start of the action.

The finished pattern may or may not resemble the shape of the person, which is not really a major requirement. What is a major requirement is that your mental focus of intent is directed towards the fact that what you are drawing is the energy grid of the recipient of the work. The full name of the person in the pattern helps with that, but your use of imagination and intent matters more. Let your hand guide you, as the source of the damage may be something different to what you think it is. As you are drawing out the patterns, you will be 'nudged' to express the damage in certain areas. Just trust that instinct and let it strengthen.

The next stage is ritual. It is very simple but important: name the pattern formally. Voice your acknowledgement of the presence of the goddess you are working with, name the pattern (I name thee x) and then ask the goddess and the beings that work with and through her to work on the pattern with you.

Once that is done, then comes the visionary work. Standing before the altar, close your eyes and 'see' the drawing using your imagination. 'See' the goddess standing on the other side of the altar and 'see' the power flowing through the pattern, and where the pattern is broken. The use of your imagination to trigger the work tells the beings and deity what it is you are trying to achieve. Ask the goddess for beings to work through you, to assist and teach you in your work. You will get the sense of beings building up behind you ready to work. Take your time with this; for some people the act of triggering magical interactions using the imagination is easy, but for others it can be very hard. Give yourself time to build up the power and intent.

Once you feel the presence behind you, look at the pattern on the altar and notice that it has become bigger and is no longer just a drawing, but has become the living pattern there on the altar with you. You will see broken patterns and weak areas. See yourself pick up the broken threads and the moment you touch the threads, you will feel arms passing through your arms and working through you. When you feel that, surrender your logic and just let your arms work.

You will find yourself weaving the damaged threads back together and reconstructing the original pattern. You will know when the job is done because the sense of beings working through you will come to an end and they will withdraw. Upon that withdrawal, open your eyes, place the drawing in a bowl and burn it, while seeing the whole pattern as a pattern of light still on the altar.

With the completed pattern of light, ask the beings who were working with you to bridge the pattern into the person or object that is being worked upon. Look into the candle that is burning before you and imagine that the completed pattern is held in the candle flame. Take your time with this step and let the pattern image build up in the flame. Once it is strong in your mind's eye, blow the flame out and voice out loud that you send the pattern to its owner and ask the beings to ensure it is properly delivered and absorbed by the person or place. If it is for yourself, as you blow out the flame, imagine the pattern flowing into you and settling within you.

Leave the candle burning on the altar and offer the weaver goddess bread, wine, water and salt in thanks for her work. If she asks for anything else, then give it to her without question or hesitation.

Weaving by Utterance

This form of magical weaving is far less ritualised and is free flowing, more 'shamanic' for want of a better word. It would be used primarily upon a patch of land that has been damaged or magically pinned/ interfered with.

The tool for this work is simply your voice. The key to the work is repetition, focus of intent (as always) and using the imagination to allow the weaver goddess or Fates to work through you. The key is visiting the land or site in person every day for a certain length of time, and the rest of the day, tuning into the space to work from a distance. So really, this technique will only work if you are living or staying close to the space.

Everyday that you walk towards the space, be aware of the deity you are working with as you walk. See them building up alongside you and their attendant beings all around you. As you arrive at the space/ land/rock, simply utter over the earth a simple one sentence declaration. It would need to be tailored to the individual circumstance, but would be something like, 'you are rewoven', or 'you are whole', 'you are strong and healthy'. Note the declaration is a positive one, not a negative one. This is of key importance: you need to instruct the pattern, the substance and the attending beings of what needs to happen.

For the rest of the day, every 30 minutes, stop what you are doing and 'see' the place in your mind's eye. Utter the declaration and then continue with your ordinary tasks. Do this all day everyday for the set length of time that you have dedicated to the task. It works like a dripping tap, putting focus and instruction for a particular thing to happen. Your focus directs the power and your declaration instructs the beings what to do, and all of this is overseen by the deity. At the end of each day thank the deity for their assistance and when the job is finished, leave her a gift by the space being worked upon.

This method of working does not directly engage the 'waves of energy' or a pattern, i.e. the magician is not directly working in vision with the energy structures to bring about change. Rather than magician is tuning into the deity that oversees that energy weave and is focussing an intent request for the deity/beings to actively engage the energy pattern; you act a link in the chain by intentional request and then bridging the action by use of utterance with intent.

As with all magical weaving, you will often not see a dramatic immediate result, though that can happen, but you will see powerful results nonetheless. Magic takes its time to filter through into a physical space and works through the natural tides of the land. But you will see the results. I have had immediate dramatic results, and other times I have had results that were powerful and defined, but took a full four seasons to manifest. One particular patch of land I worked upon was a massacre site that still had all the fear, rage and mental imbalance churning within the land. The area was renowned for being devoid of birds and creatures: nothing would go there.

Firstly I opened the gates to death to shepherd through the remaining spirits that were still trapped upon the land. Next I worked to reweave the pattern of that patch of land and to unhook the pattern of death/disaster from the substance of the land. I did that by working with utterance, and then more directly in vision using a weaving action in collaboration with the weaver goddess I was working with. Finally I opened the gates again and called in the directional elements to 're-set' the land.

Within days of finishing the work the birds returned, deer were spotted, the trees started to look healthier energetically; it was a joy to see. Within a year it was totally transformed and had gone from a place that local people shunned to a place where children went to play, flocks of birds sat and chattered, and wild flowers were springing up all over the place. The key elements that brought such success were not the power of the magician or anything egotistical like that. What brought about the success were simple magical dynamics: it was the right time, the right weaver goddess and the right intent; it was like popping a boil. We are the minor players and simple catalysts that come along at just the right time; nature and the inner worlds had already done their part but what was needed was a human catalyst with intent to bring about rebalance. When the damage is caused by humans, it is humans who must instigate the healing process.

Water

Similar types of work can be done with water, i.e. sacred utterance over water and then returning the water to the river or stream so that it can spread out and work upon the land as well as the waterways. This is a very diffuse way of working and can be used for the healing of vast tracks of land, and because water often goes underground, it can also affect change at a very deep level not only for the land but for the ancestral consciousness of the land also.

The techniques would be very simple, with again the key being focus of intent, relevant deity, repeated utterance or sound etc. Just remember that water is immensely powerful and that once something is poured into the river, it will replicate over and over until the pattern has spread out across the whole land mass that the river touches. Keeping that in mind it is important that the intention for healing is kept very simple and to the point. It would also bode well to commune with the consciousness or deity of the river first to ask if they actually need or want your help. Often what we see as being a toxic damaged river is actually already under some natural process of change or repair, so check first before you dive into the picture to save the world. It might not want saving!

Summary

The magical action of weaving has endless applications and possibilities from externalised action to deep formless inner action, and the more you work with it, the more you will recognise it in magical texts, mythical stories and cultural application. Old songs passed down from generation to generation that are about protection are a form of magical weaving; through the pattern that the song produces, a weave of ancestral protection is developed and passed from mother to child.

Songs sung while women literally weave, particularly traditional songs about the family, the children, the land etc are woven into the fabric as they weave. That fabric would then make up the marriage bedding for a new family and the song would be embedded within the fabric.

At the other end of the magical spectrum, Kabbalists working in vision within the Tree of Life, particularly at the edge of the Abyss, often work to weave power and consciousness within the angelic patterns of physical manifestation. It is a key element of magical work and is one that is sadly overlooked.

The examples I have given you are just the tip of the iceberg for this form of magical work and most of magical weaving has to be individually discovered and developed. It is not a hard fast technique that can be easily passed along through text as much depends upon the traits and abilities of the individual magician, their culture, the strength of their imagination and the weaver goddess that flows through their land.

You have to experiment and find ways to work that are appropriate for you. The main step is to find the right deity to work with: there are many weaver goddesses and various cultural expressions of the Fates, but it has to be the ones who work strongly through your own land. Every land has a version; just find yours. Don't choose by fashion, i.e. 'oh I will work with Ariadne because I love all that Greek stuff'... look into the cultural/religious/mythical patterns within your own land and bloodlines and see what comes up. Look in myth and legend, but also reach in vision into the land itself to see what presents; you can often be surprised by what emerges. That will work the strongest for you.

As magicians it is always important for us to push boundaries: experiment, be curious and be constantly willing to learn, to be surprised and to be humbled.

Appendix

1 - The Magical Understanding of Good and Evil

When walking a magical path the practitioner soon comes up against issues of good v evil, duality of power, left hand path etc which can bring to the surface a great many questions that we have to ask of both ourselves and those involved. I feel it is important for us as magicians to step outside of the dogmas and beliefs inherent within our culture and society, which are often deep seated and not immediately apparent to us. By doing so it enables us to ascertain what is actually happening, why, and how to find a way to navigate through issues in a way that compliments who we are and what we are trying to achieve.

What we perceive as good or evil largely depends on our system of beliefs, be they religious, cultural, philosophical etc, and our own emotional development. It also is deeply effected by our own needs both in personal development and everyday living.

Our systems of belief and the wider religious/cultural pattern in which we were born and raised have a massive effect upon how we view the world. As children we accept such dogmas without question, particularly if raised in a religious household. As teens we rebel against such dogmas and begin the process of questioning. Often though, the questioning element of our personal development can become limited by a continued unconscious adherence to the dogmatic pattern which results in not necessarily breaking away from the pattern, but a continuing rebellion against a dogma which in turn feeds and strengthens it.

We can see this for example in the work of Crowley. I am not an expert on Crowley by any means, and am commenting from the outside looking in. But it is an example that is known by most people in the magical arena. Crowley was raised in a very strict and unhealthy Christian household that was mired in the sexually repressed Victorian era with all its inherent behavioural imbalances. Crowley struck out to try and become the opposite of what he had been raised in. This eventually brought about a huge change in thinking, but his reasoning was still mired within the dogma of Christianity, just from an opposing point of view.

At that time, I think it would have been nearly impossible for someone of his time, culture and background to have completely stepped out of that pattern. But in his struggle, whether we agree with it or not, he and others like him broke down barriers that our generation no longer has to bother with, and yet many branches of magic still cling to that outworn pattern. And therein lies one of the problems: we have become so used to working and evolving within the pattern that we forget that we are now able to step outside of the pattern rather than being the antithesis of the pattern. We become stuck in the white magician, black magician, left hand and right hand path mentality.

So how do we operate? I think the first step for a magician is to know their own personal limitations of what they are and are not willing to do and take responsibility for. On one hand, the more 'spiritually' inclined magician is likely to have a set of heroic ethics that they vigorously defend, often without direct experience, and postulate to others about. Over time, with the dedication of a magical path, the magician is then put into a variety of life situations that directly challenge not only the validity of those ethics, but also the ability of the individual to make more informed decisions regarding their ethics. Some are realised to be empty shells of dogmatic or fanciful beliefs, and some are discovered to be of vast importance. That distinction also strengthens the magician and enables them to uphold the important ethics in the face of extreme challenge.

Slowly, the ethics or concepts that may be considered admirable by many societies are put to the practical test but many fall by the wayside as the magician realises their futility. Others prove to be difficult to uphold, but wonderful boundaries that bring out the best in someone. This is a filter mechanism that most of us have been through in one way or another, so that when we emerge battered and still standing a few decades later, we have a much more realistic idea of what we can and cannot do, and more importantly what were truly are willing or not willing to do to survive.

It is easy to stand in judgement of someone from a safe vantage point and feel good about ourselves. But once fate tosses us the ravages of a harsh life, then we begin to feel a lot more compassion and understanding for those whom we observe to be struggling against themselves or their society. We know, because we have been there. So a dawning of understanding of the hardship of true survival lights our path.

Similarly in the other direction, following a magical path of selfishness, of using power purely and unashamedly for the pursuit of wants and needs gives freedom to the magician who has lived in a stifling family/society. Self-indulgence and self-preservation gives a sense of power, a sense of control of our own lives and destinies. We gain a sense of our own power and importance. Until it begins to go wrong and then the dawning of how limited we are as beings happens, and how wants and needs do not fill a greater sense of identity nor do they teach us truly about power. Our addictions begin to rule and then destroy, to weaken and expose the false sense of security that was gained.

I began my magical path with a terrible sense of self-righteousness. I asked the inner contacts for learning, for wisdom, for experience (not always such a great idea). I certainly got what I asked for and was thrown to the wolves. Every pedestal I took delight in standing upon was knocked over until I understood the dilemmas of those I had so arrogantly looked down upon in my youth. It is a terribly hard long and painful lesson, but that is what magic does. It confronts you: it is the path of Hercules.

Eventually I learned and am still learning to look beyond the 'pattern' of what I personally consider 'ethical', and to recognise my own weaknesses and failures in the cold hard light of day. I realise now this process will never end, which is good as it means we can constantly grow, evolve and learn.

Knowing our own limitations is a very important part of the development of magic within us and has great bearing upon how we wield that magic. The rules of engagement in life are the same for magic, from the small aspects to the greatest ones. So consider for example, eating meat. It is easy to buy a pre packed, chopped and ready to cook bit of meat. It is not so easy to look into the eyes of an animal and watch it die by your own hands. So many people say, "I could not kill an animal, but I eat meat". Others will state that any eating of meat is cruel and 'unspiritual'.

It is a statement that is easy to make in some countries where there is a social safety net, or access to vegetarian protein sources, so although some may go hungry from time to time, people do not die of starvation. We have that choice and often choose not to kill – our ethics are a product of our living circumstances.

But put in a situation where there is no safety net, and you are very hungry, your children are hungry and if you do not kill an animal there is a good chance that you may starve, then it is a different matter. The will to survive is all encompassing. It does not make the killing any easier, but it makes it necessary: that is the reality, the true reality of nature that we are often protected from in modern society. That luxury enables us to be ethical: but magic begins when we know our limitations, we know what we are really capable of doing, both for good and bad under extreme circumstances. Then and only then can we begin to understand power in a magical context and learn how to navigate our way through the maze.

So back to good and evil. What do those words actually mean anyway? We bandy then around in religion, in spirituality and in magical paths. But do we really understand what they mean? What is evil? Is it evil to maim and kill? Is it evil to destroy? It all depends on where you are in context to the power. As humans, we find genocide against other humans as intolerable, evil incarnate. But we commit such acts without thought on a regular basis against other creatures. Is mass murder evil? If someone kills a load of seals, or ponies or kittens, we consider that evil, and inhuman. But if they are cows or pigs, then it serves our purpose and is therefore acceptable. So evil in reality is something we do not like to happen to us either as individuals or as a species.

High or powerful magic is like wielding nuclear power, it can do great damage over a long period of time. The power itself is neither good nor evil, but its use can have devastating effects regardless of the intention behind it. It is a dangerous tool and the more power a magician is able to access the more damage or good they can potentially do with it. How that power is applied is directly related to how that magician perceives themselves and the world around them.

Because of that dynamic, what often happens is a dynamic whereby the more potential for power a magician has, the greater/ more turbulent their life experiences will be in order to bring them to a relative mature place, or to switch them off – a bit like blowing a fuse. Those who do not have the capacity for mediating large amounts of power tend to have a more stable constant life experience (unless of course they have already got their shit together, which is almost unheard of). This dynamic seems to run in relation to the capacity of the person/path for power.

It is something that has happened to me and something I have also observed many times over in other magicians. There is no sense of any paternalistic teaching parent god in the dynamic; it is more a matter of power in, power out, in the weave of life. The trick is to recognise what is happening and engage the process for learning and strengthening, rather than flailing around in the dark and cursing the gods (Been there, done that).

When the dynamic first really kicked in for me, I was horrified that suddenly life was throwing me big balls of dangerous shit on an almost daily basis that was getting beyond silly. Luckily there was an elder magician around in my wider community that pointed out to me that every damn thing I was going through was directly challenging me on my stance of ethics, of understanding and of limitations.

That was a major turning point not only in my coping strategy, but also in my magical understanding and development. I began to engage directly with each challenge to draw what I could from the situations and turn them into learning curves, strengthening exercises and humble pie eating sessions. The more I engaged, the wider the door of magical contact became. I began to see the 'bad' side of life and magic as something that balanced out and polished the 'good' side. I began to see the dynamic of how creative magical power needed to exist in the presence of destructive magical power; instead of trying to get rid of the bad power, it is merely balanced out by a creative power or is engaged with intent to redress imbalance and visa versa.

Like everything else, you can read about something or be taught about something until the cows come home, but the true deeper meanings and the visceral understanding of magic cannot really take seed and grow until it is a direct learning experience.

So for example this chapter is not really written to teach, nor even to burble about my own opinions/expressions, but to open the door as that elder did for me and say, 'hey it's ok, your life is in meltdown but don't panic, this is what is happening and this is how you deal with it to survive and grow stronger'. It is a path that thousands have trodden before us, and knowing that it is a path that is not only survived, but will bring you to a wonderful dawning of deep magic is a lifeline that can light your way in the darkest of times.

2 - Understanding the Void and the Inner Worlds

There has been a lot of confusion in various magical discussions at conferences and online as to what certain words mean when they are used in terms of magical visionary work. The two biggest questions that tend to arise repeatedly are: What is the Void? What are the Inner Worlds? Hopefully this clears such questions up!

What are the Inner Worlds?

The inner worlds are states of energy and consciousness that exist outside and independent of the human body. They are not a product of our collective imagination however our collective imagination over millennia has created 'interfaces' or images by which we can understand and interact with the various forces that exist all around us. These energies are the forces of the universe, the templates of creation and destruction, and some are energetic constructs that humanity has built and worked within throughout our history.

Through visionary work we can interact with various beings such as angelic beings, land spirits, deities, demonic beings, the dead etc. We find these beings in various inner realms, for example the realm of death, the Underworld, the angelic realm, the desert/Tree of Life, inner temples etc.

We can also plunge deeper into the inner worlds to experience and interact with the forces of nature, of life and death and of Divinity itself. This interaction is not new and has been used in various ways by tribal magicians, ancient priests, mystics and visionaries from various cultures throughout time.

In the West we slowly became divorced from this method of working for a variety of reasons from cultural beliefs, religious dogma, scientific rationalism etc. This divorce has had a massive impact on magical practice in the West and we are only recently starting to slowly recover from that severing.

Bear in mind that the use of these words is my usage that I learned. Other traditions that still work in these areas sometimes use different names, but the place is the same, so it is important to understand the place itself and its function rather than just get hung up on the name.

The Void

The void itself is the most commonly misunderstood term used in visionary magic. Some think of it as the Biblical Abyss, some think it is the 'astral realms' and some think it describes their head the morning after a bottle of whisky.

The void is a place of nothingness that holds the potential for everything: it is like the universe drawing breath before it breathes life into existence. Everything comes from the void into manifestation; it is the raw power of potential, when the energy has gathered to create and is just on the threshold of the process of manifestation. For Kabbalists, it is the power of Divine utterance/potential as it begins its parade down the Tree of Life, taking its form from interacting with the spheres of power before finally manifesting in Malkuth.

In visionary magical terms the void can be worked with in two key ways. The first way to develop a method for working with the void is to imagine the void as a place of nothingness that lies beyond a threshold: we imagine a flame, we pass through the flame using the element of fire as a gateway, and we pass into a place where there is no time, no movement, nothing.

As the student gets used to being in a place where there is nothing and being able to have a still and silent mind, they have acquired the ability to 'work' with the void. Because the void is full of all potential, it can be used as a stepping through point or threshold to gain access to other places. It is also a very good tool to use to slow the mind down so that clear work can begin. You can step through the void, and you also experience the void by having your mind totally still and silent.

The next phase of working with the void is to bring the void into yourself, or better said, to 'tune' yourself to the void. Instead of stepping over a threshold to the void, simply sit and slowly silence your mind and body until you are nowhere and nothing. Within that silence you focus upon the void as the place that all potential and creation comes from: the shift from being still and silent to awareness of the void as the energy from which everything flows, moves your consciousness from simple stillness to being 'within the void'. This in turn prepares the magician to be able to bridge and mediate power from unformed potential to manifest form.

That shift of awareness is a major tool in magic and allows the deeper powers within you to rise to the surface while plugging you into the power frequency of creation, the power potential that is within everything that is physically manifest. Everything is constantly creating and destroying at an energetic level in some form or other and the use of the void shifts you into that stream of power and consciousness.

It is not an easy thing to do and some people take months to learn the technique, some take years and others can master it in weeks. It is a very individual experience but it never stops deepening and developing: the power of the void within you deepens and grows throughout your working life as a magician until it becomes an extremely profound and powerful experience.

It really depends upon your own mind, the environment in which you live and also the external input your mind receives on a daily basis. For someone who is used to living in a very simple way, the void is not too difficult a task for them to achieve. For someone raised around computers, fast bites of information, TV, phones etc, it can be much harder for them to master the stillness. But it is not impossible. The longer your attention span, the easier it gets.

The void can be used as a threshold; it can also be a place to work if you are working on a magical task that involves mediating a new power, energy etc into the manifest world. It is also extremely useful if you are magically attacked by a powerful being: when you go in the void, your boundaries loosen which enables you to spread out your consciousness to everything that is around you... you become like mist which in turn creates a situation where the being has nothing to grab onto. Comes in very handy!

Stilling the Monkey Mind...Why?

It is very important, particularly with visionary magic, but really, in all magic, that the mind can be properly stilled and silenced. Once that has been achieved, then the magician can learn to use their mind with absolute focus to achieve magical patterns, inner contact and hold/mediate power without distraction. The mind is the major tool of the magician and a monkey mind is a disaster in magic.

Meditation, working with the void and learning focussed simple ritual are all ways that a magician learns to harness their mind and imagination to work with it. Magic is about moving around energy and power; it is interacting with other beings through consciousness,

so a trained mind is absolutely essential. The longer term training of
the mind in magic also begins the process of 're wiring' the brain so
that the brain learns the magical skills in detail, learns to recognise and
work with the magical images or vocabulary in depth, which in turn
allows the magician to do his or her job.

It is exactly the same as learning a detailed skill such as a classical
art, or master carpentry or a science at a doctorate level. The brain
has to adjust itself to develop specific skills that only long term work
and study develop. This is why instant magic manuals, ritual recipe
books etc do not make a magician: constant work and training in
specific areas of inner and outer work make a magician.

Being aware of how much of a monkey your mind really is can
be a bit of a shock. Just test it by sitting in a room with no stimulus:
no noise, no people, nothing to look at. Sit in the silence and be aware
of your thoughts. See how your mind jumps from one thing to the
next, how much your body wants to move; it can be quite a revelation.
Then shut your eyes and sit silently. Again be aware of thoughts, and
movements that the body tries to make: we are very rarely silent in
our modern world.

Once you are aware of the level of monkey mind you possess,
then you can start to slowly train the mind to settle, to be quiet, for
the body to be still and not itch, move, twitch. Don't try to force it
too much in a determined 'I am going to conquer myself' way. Just
practice once or twice a day to be silent for a short while and slowly
let that time build up until you can sit in silence for a long time without
realising how much time has passed.

With that achieved, begin work with the two different levels of
the void visions to see how different the two states of silence feel.
One is simple silence and stillness. The other is silence and stillness

but with a huge sense of power behind it. That is the creation potential that is in the void.

The next stage is to practice walking around the house and down the street in a state of inner silence. This exercise is harder, but it is the initial training for empowered ritual: ritual performed while the mind is in the inner worlds. You learn to be in two places at once, with the mind in the inner temple or in a specific inner realm while the body is conducting a ritual action. The power begins to flow from the inner world through you and out into the ritual. That ritual forming of power is then mediated out into the world in whatever form you are working on.

Index

Josephine McCarthy's Magical Knowledge Trilogy

Order direct from

online at - www.mandrake.uk.net

Email: mandrake@mandrake.uk.net

Lightning Source UK Ltd.
Milton Keynes UK
UKOW02f1009011215

263831UK00001B/52/P